MW00596401

PROVING GOD

*Triumphant Living
Through Tithing*

PROVING GOD

Triumphant Living
Through Tithing

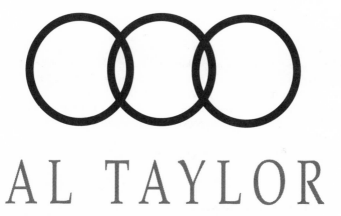

AL TAYLOR

Scripture quotations are taken from the following sources: *The Amplified Bible (Amp)*. Old Testament copyright © 1965, 1987 by The Zondervan Corporation. The Amplified New Testament copyright © 1958, 1987 by The Lockman Foundation. Used by permission. *The Holy Bible, New King James Version (NKJV)*. Copyright © 1979, 1980, 1982 by Thomas Nelson, Inc., Nashville, TN. Used by permission.

ISBN: 0-87148-954-6

Library of Congress Catalog Card Number: 91-060310

Copyright © 1991
PATHWAY PRESS
Cleveland, Tennessee 37311
All Rights Reserved

Printed in the United States of America

DEDICATION

I dedicate this book to my dear wife, Brenda. She has served as God's illustration to me of the joy one can have through totally releasing everything to the lordship of Jesus. Her pursuit of God through His Word, through prayer and through service to others is an ever-present challenge to my own weak efforts. She is always cheerfully busy proving God by giving herself in ministry to Christ and to the people for whom He died.

Contents

CONTENTS

INTRODUCTION

God said He wanted you to prove Him—prove Him to yourself, to those around you and to the world. The apostle Paul confirmed this concept in the New Testament when he said, "And be not conformed to this world: but be ye transformed by the renewing of your mind, that ye may prove what is that good, and acceptable, and perfect, will of God" (Romans 12:2).

The world cannot see God except as He is revealed in your life. The world cannot understand God's Word except as you illustrate its power in you. You are God's proof. Therefore, we who know Him must be the most convincing proof imaginable. We know how good and gracious He is. We know His Word is true. It brought to us the wonderful relationship that Jesus called the new birth.

When Malachi wrote God's command, "Prove me now herewith," he was addressing a generation much like our own. Materialism was rampant. Divorce was up. Many church leaders were backslidden. The Temple suffered both neglect and abuse. "Good is evil and evil is good" was a theme then as now, and it wearied the Lord.

God promised judgment against the sorcerers, the adulterers, the false swearers and those who oppressed the defenseless, such as widows, orphans, strangers and those who worked for wages. He also promised to deal with those who do not fear God. Had God not been unchangeable, they would have been consumed by His judgment.

The Jews responded to God's message. They wanted to know how to return to God, and God immediately addressed their practice of robbing Him in tithes and offerings. He apprised them that they were indeed cursed for this sin. Then He offered space to repent. His amazing grace came pouring

9

out. Revival came with genuine financial reform as the first step in repentance.

I believe His offer to return to Him the same way still stands for this generation. God gives us opportunity to prove both His truthfulness and His desire to bless. He has promised to forgive in response to true repentance. He has promised that obedience will be blessed. Faithfulness in tithing and giving will bring prosperity, and the world will see proof of God's power and goodness. He will rebuke the devourer and prove to us that He is both provider and protector.

Does the ancient practice of tithing still bring blessing to those who tithe in our day? How does it work? What does it mean? Why is there so much confusion on this subject? Why has the church been timid in dealing with this powerful principle? We will attempt to answer these questions and release the power of God through faith in His Word and by faithfulness to obey as stewards of the King.

Why does God use the believer as His proof? Because the world cannot understand the Word of God. Why does He use money as His illustration? Because the world is more interested in money than any other thing. When the unbeliever sees that the Christian response to money is so different from his own, his curiosity is aroused. When he sees you live the principles of God's Word, he has an opportunity to see the gospel revealed in flesh. When he sees your freedom, he wishes for freedom too.

We love God through our obedience. We love others through our demonstration of God's truth. Proving God is an awesome blessing to the prover and to the observer.

We are blessed to be a blessing.

Al Taylor

10

CHAPTER 1

MAGNIFICENT PURPOSE

Fulfilled in You

God had you in mind when He purposed this magnificent creation. He declares in Genesis 1:26, "And God said, Let us make man in our image, after our likeness: and let them have dominion." Think of it! God who has all power, all knowledge, all wisdom; God who had already created a beautiful universe; God who had millions of angels to do His will and keep Him company still wanted you! He wanted you to be His child. Like any proud parent, He wanted you to *look* like Him and *be* like Him. He wants you to call Him *Father*!

It is the most normal thing for human parents to search for their own reflection in the countenance of their child. Nothing can give those parents any greater satisfaction than to see that image mature in the child day by day. And so, we can take delight that God has committed His unlimited resources to give us the opportunity to see His purpose fulfilled in us. He gives each of us the opportunity to see His image in us and to see it grow and mature day by day.

After God created man, He gave him a command which would enable him to participate in that great purpose. He said, "Be fruitful, and multiply, and replenish the earth, and subdue it" (Genesis 1:28).

Now the first part of that command was identical to the one He had given to the animals: "Be fruitful, and multiply."

one He had given to the animals: "Be fruitful, and multiply." The animals have no choice but to obey the word of God's command. We refer to their obedience as instinct. But the truth is, they are obeying the word of God's command. That makes them fruitful and therefore qualified to reproduce. Disobedience would interfere with their fruitfulness and threaten their species with extinction.

God's command to us was the same in that first phrase, but we have the choice to obey or disobey. I can only be fruitful in the divine sense through obedience to His Word. The Holy Spirit will then produce the fruit of the Spirit around that seed (Word) in my life. Nature illustrates it over and over: Fruit is formed around seed. Spiritual fruit is a manifestation of the nature of God the Father. It is always formed around our commitment to His Word (the seed—Matthew 13:23).

This fruitfulness in our lives brings glory to God (John 15:8) because it fulfills His purpose that we should be in His image. We can only be in His image as His nature is revealed in us through fruitfulness. Then we are ready to multiply.

Look at what is happening to people who reject God's Word and His fruitfulness. Instead of multiplying, they kill their babies. Instead of building families, they try to enjoy sex without commitment. Those who don't break up their families or kill their babies have lives that are spiritually barren as the consequence of their rejecting the Word of God.

Some Dominion

God also said He would give us dominion. He has all dominion, but He gives you and me some dominion. This provides the opportunity for me to exercise my free will to show Him that I agree with His purpose, that I want to be like Him. The area of dominion given to me is my area of stewardship. I am a trustee over what He has placed in my care. He tells me how to use those resources, but He gives me the privilege to obey or disobey. Obedience will produce likeness. Disobedience will cause me to take on the likeness of God's ugly enemy.

Just as every responsible parent begins to train each of

his children by assigning tasks and requiring accountability, so does our all-wise heavenly Father to each of us. He gives us the delightful opportunity to cooperate with His purpose and experience fulfillment, to see our trusteeship grow, and to see our capacity to love Him and enjoy His presence constantly increase.

When man disobeyed God, he experienced spiritual death just as God had warned. Before the disobedience Adam wanted for nothing. He had no worries. The home God had prepared included everything imaginable to satisfy man's needs. Then every day in the cool of the evening God walked with His family, Adam and Eve, through this beautiful garden. They enjoyed fellowship with the Creator. Their greatest need was thus fulfilled—and God's purpose to have His own family and to enjoy fellowship with that family was also being satisfied.

The very day he sinned, man no longer looked forward to fellowship with God. Instead, he ran and hid. Sinners are still trying to hide from God. They hide with drugs, devil music, denial, materialism, false beliefs, and so on. They will try anything in hope of staying out of His sight.

Perhaps you have noticed how the business of sewing leaves is booming again. Adam and Eve tried to make their own covering with leaves. That adequately symbolizes man's religions. They all have no more efficacy to meet our spiritual need than Adam's drying, shrinking, scratching covering of leaves could cover his nakedness and hide his shame.

God was not taken by surprise. He foreknew man's fall and provided for it. Neither would God's purpose be thwarted. He began to work with man under the new set of circumstances. He provided a comfortable covering for Adam and Eve. He increased Eve's conception so that His family would still be produced in spite of those who exercised their free will to opt out of God's purpose and forfeit being part of God's family.

The Power of Choice

For you to really be like God requires the ability and the

opportunity to exercise free will. God gave us that capacity. He also had a planet where there existed a rebel spirit named Lucifer. So God placed man on that planet, which provided an option. We serve God, therefore, because we choose Him, not because there is no choice.

The Garden of Eden was man's first home on planet Earth. It was such a beautiful place! The animals were contented and cared for. The trees were healthy and fruitful. Flowers were abundant. Everything man needed was there. The choice was there too.

Two Trees

In the middle of the garden stood two opposite trees. One was the Tree of Life; the other, the tree of death. God invited Adam and Eve to eat from the Tree of Life and live. His instructions were clear: Do not eat from the Tree of Knowledge of Good and Evil. If you do, you will die.

Eve added to God's words. She said if we touch that tree, we will die. Many people have been caught in this trap. By adding to God's Word we presume we are making ourselves safer. Our words have neither the wisdom, power, nor the life of God's Word. Once we have added to God's Word, Satan only has to break our words to make us doubt or disobey God's Word. We are not to add to nor take away from God's Word. We are to receive it and obey it.

The two trees hold great symbolism. The Tree of Life, for example, is still with us. The cross upon which Jesus died has become a Tree of Life. God invites everyone to eat from this tree. But just as our forefathers failed to accept His invitation to eat and live forever, most people decline to partake of Christ and live.

The tree that was forbidden is the one we all try first. This tree represents a choice to go man's way. That choice still produces death as the consequence of our rebellion. It is a powerful illustration of the vital role of stewardship in the fulfillment of God's purpose in us.

Adam was given responsibility to dress and keep the

garden for its owner. He was given permission to eat as much as he wanted from all that was available, with one exception. That one exception was a symbol of God's ownership. The owner had the right to authorize the use of His property, and He had the right to forbid its use or to restrict its use.

Adam as steward had no ownership. Stewards are not owners. Stewards do not have inherent rights. They have responsibility. They have user rights as defined by the owner. And they have accountability to the owner.

Adam failed in his stewardship. He failed to obey the owner's instructions. He exercised his dominion—his freedom of choice. He indulged himself, and he had to give an account. He had to pay the consequences.

Man is still failing in the pattern of Adam. We are all stewards. God is still the owner. The Bible speaks His instruction to us, and we are accountable to God. We will be judged by His Word.

God still maintains a symbol of His ownership—the tithe. Like the forbidden tree standing in the midst of the garden, the tithe stands in the midst of all material possessions entrusted to you. As Adam was instructed not to consume the forbidden fruit, you and I are forbidden to consume the tithe. All the trees were under Adam's care, including the one from which he was forbidden to eat. All the material possessions entrusted to you are in your care. But the tithe in the midst of it is not legally available for your consumption. It is the mark of God's ownership.

We can only cooperate with God and His magnificent purpose when we view things from His perspective. He is God. He is Creator. All things were created by Him. They all belong to Him. He created man. We belong to Him. His purpose for us is amazingly great and wonderful. It can only be realized by us as we submit to Him and His Word.

We can only have the correct perspective, we can only know the truth, when we accept God's Word regarding things—material possessions. He has entrusted to us certain resources. He has directed their proper use. Obedience contributes to His purpose for us, which is life. Disobedience frustrates His purpose and produces death.

God created the material realm that is part of His plan. We are His highest creation, and our development during natural life is linked to learning how to obey His Word through the proper use of things. He is delighted for us to benefit from the use of material possessions. Christ declared that it is the Father's good pleasure to give us the Kingdom (Luke 12:32).

After man's fall, his tendency has been to deal with his insecurity by accumulating an abundance of things. No matter how much he gathers, he will never have enough if his security depends upon the abundance of things. One of the major benefits we receive from returning the tithe is the constant reminder that God is our source and our security. Each time Adam and Eve looked upon the beautiful Garden of Eden there stood the reminder that it belonged to God and He had defined the terms of its use by that which was withheld from their consumption. Everything He entrusts to us arrives with the tithe in it as a reminder of His ownership.

Without that correct perspective regarding the material realm, the truth of where we fit into the spectrum of God's purpose eludes us. He then appears too small for our source. Things seem too important. And we consume the forbidden, which leads us to death. Death is the consequence of disobedience, of losing the truth. God wants us to have life. Life always accompanies compliance with the truth.

JESUS IS PROPRIETOR

Observing His Lordship

Stanley Tam is a Christian businessman from Lima, Ohio. Because of his special dedication of his life to Christ, he is often asked to speak publicly. On one such occasion after he had completed his message, he invited the people to come to the front for a time of prayer. As they were praying, he leaned across the lectern to pray with them.

At that point God spoke to him and instructed him to give the full ownership of his business to God. Stanley reacted, "Well, God, I have already given you half of my business. I don't know anyone else who has done that much. My wife owns 25 percent, and I own 25 percent. Do you want her share too?" God responded that He wanted it all.

Upon returning home Stanley shared with his wife what had happened. Then he asked her how she felt about giving God all of her shares in their company. She responded, "If God wants it, give it to Him."

When Stanley explained to his attorney what God had instructed him to do, the attorney thought he had lost his mind. Through persistence he finally found an attorney who was willing to help him carry out this strange idea.

The transfer was eventually completed. God owned all the stock, and He would receive all the profits. Stanley would serve as president and receive a salary like the other employees of the company.

Stanley admitted he was tempted to feel proud of what he had done. But in only a few months the successful company was performing markedly better. It didn't take long for it to become the largest company of its kind in America, perhaps the largest in the world. Its president now readily admits that the new owner is unbelievably smart. He knows the solution to every problem. And that company has now given millions of dollars for the work of the church.

There is another dimension to this story. Stanley experienced a new freedom after he gave away the company. He didn't have to worry about the business anymore. He discovered a new freedom in his personal soulwinning. In prayer he asked the Lord to give him one soul per day for a year. At the end of the year, he had 365 names recorded who had accepted Christ. God had answered his prayer.

He prayed again for an increased harvest of souls. This time he asked God for two souls per day for the coming year. When that year ended, he could count 730 new names of people who had prayed with him to accept Christ. He was so delighted and fulfilled that he dared to ask God for more. This time he asked for three souls per day for the coming year. When I met Stanley at a convention of the National Association of Evangelicals (NAE) in Columbus, Ohio, he testified that so far that year God had been giving him three souls per day.

Your Confession

Anyone who knows Christ is thrilled to see God's purpose demonstrated so dramatically. However, you made a similar commitment to Christ when you were saved—not for three souls a day in soulwinning but that you were giving everything to Him. Your first response is probably "I don't remember that" and "How would you know anyway?" The only reason I know you did is that it is required in the Word of God.

The apostle Paul said in Romans 10:9, 10 that if we

18

would confess with our mouths and believe in our hearts that Jesus is Lord, we would be saved. That is the procedure for accepting Christ. It is an agreement with God the Father that Jesus is Lord: He says Jesus is Lord (Psalm 110:1; Matthew 22:44). When I say it and believe it, a miraculous transformation called the new birth occurs. If you are born again, then you call Jesus Lord.

And what does *Lord* mean? It is an ancient term not in wide usage today. However, renters still use it when they refer to the landlord. Of course, we know they are referring to the one who owns the property. And that is the proper sense of the term *Lord*. Jesus is Savior, Master and owner (1 Corinthians 15:27; Hebrews 1:2). When I believe in Him and call Him my Lord, I am submitting willfully to God's order of things. I am confessing that He owns me and everything entrusted to me. After that there should be no question of my joyful obedience to Him. I can give up anything and everything at His direction, because when I accepted Him, I gave it all up to Him that very moment. If I am saddened when Christ directs me to give up or give away any material possession, then I have forgotten I had already given it to Him. It is His to use as He pleases. My joy is to come from the opportunity to serve Him in the giving as well as in the possessing.

Your banker is a fair illustration of this concept. He is your trustee, or steward. The money you deposit is not the property of the banker, although he has possession of it. You would be alarmed if your banker became downcast every time you wrote a check or made a withdrawal. You would know he had an unhealthy view of your property.

Typically, you make deposits and withdrawals at your bank. If the banker gives a proper accounting of your funds and has a good attitude toward you and your property, then the relationship grows and improves. Your trust and confidence increase. You become willing to trust him with more.

God owns everything. He created it. Even in earth's fallen condition, it still belongs to God. He proclaims His ownership both in the Old and New Testaments (Psalm 24:1; 1 Corinthians 10:26, 28).

We are His stewards or trustees. We do not have

19

owner's rights. We have a steward's responsibility. We are to acknowledge His ownership: thus, we call Him Lord. We are to obey His instructions: hence, we study His Word. We must give an accounting: therefore, we bring the tithe. We will give a final report one day: for that reason, we must stay current in our management responsibilities.

Yes, it is serious business. But we have the delightful opportunity to become more like our Father through this business relationship. It is the privilege to know Him better by working with Him. He not only has us as family, He has also brought us into the family business.

Can you imagine anything so awesome? The great God and Father wanted you to be His child. He desired that you should be in His family. He also wants you to work in His business. He wants you to grow. Learn how to listen to the voice of His Spirit. Learn how to manage money and resources. Ultimately He wants us to inherit the business and His possessions with our older brother, Jesus (Romans 8:17). For now we are learning how to obey . . . how to be faithful.

Freedom and Faithfulness

We have looked briefly at God's purpose for us and at proprietorship. Our lives are made much richer simply by understanding these two fundamentals. Because they are so important to us and because the Scriptures reveal so much, let's probe a little deeper.

God's purpose appeared to be lost at the time Adam and Eve failed in their stewardship responsibility. Man could no longer walk with God each day. He was driven out of his beautiful paradise. He had to work hard to earn his living by the sweat of his brow.

Eve was placed under the authority of her husband. She would suffer greatly in childbearing. Her life would also be filled with hard labor and heartache.

Worse yet, because of sin they were separated from God. They were spiritually dead. And they would eventually die physically. Death was at work in them. It was a sad day for them and for us.

But when our Father purposes to do something, He doesn't give up. He is all-wise, all-powerful, all-knowing.

In the midst of this despair, He announced that from the seed of woman a Savior would come and defeat our enemy. He would crush the serpent's head. He would restore God's magnificent purpose! He would do away with death.

The first son born to Adam and Eve revealed the tragedy of their disobedience. Cain was born to grow up and become the first murderer. He had the fallen nature of his parents. When they disobeyed, they became unfruitful. When they multiplied, they reproduced after their kind.

Their second son, Abel, had a heart for God. He was the first prophet (Luke 11:50, 51). His worship revealed a message and an understanding of things present and things to come. God's message of redemption through sacrifice and substitution was delivered to the first family through this second son.

The two brothers also illustrate the two families in the earth. Enmity has always existed between those who are of their father the devil and those whose Father is the living God. The struggle continues this very day and is intensifying.

Adam's fall abruptly halted the development of God's fruitful nature in him. Instead, he began to develop the nature of Satan. The works of the flesh (Galatians 5:19-21) are nothing more than the nature of Satan being manifest in a human life. The fruit of the Spirit (vv. 22, 23) is none other than the nature of God being manifest in the life of the believer.

When a baby is born, it bears the image of its biological parents. As the child matures, the image becomes more pronounced. God's great wisdom was shared with fallen man each time He spoke to us of the coming Messiah. God would remedy this marring of His image in man. He would fulfill His original purpose for man through the work of the Savior.

CHAPTER 3

PURPOSE
AND
PROCESS

Christ the Key

"In whom [Christ] are hid all the treasures of wisdom and knowledge" (Colossians 2:3). Jesus declared Himself to be "the way, the truth, and the life" (John 14:6). Truth is not a concept you can simply write down. Truth is the person of our Lord himself. Throughout this study we will depend upon the principle that Christ is truth to enable us to develop an understanding of stewardship. What does the Word of God say, and how does it relate to Christ? In Him we will find the treasures of wisdom and knowledge.

Image

The apostle Paul penned a beautiful insight concerning image in Romans 8:29, 30. Amazingly, the church has argued about these verses so persistently until we have all but obscured the message. Now look: "For whom he did foreknow, he also did predestinate to be conformed to the image of his Son." There we have the New Testament provision for the fulfillment of God's original statement of purpose for us. Jesus provided the opportunity for us to be born again. Image of the parent comes with birth. We are not born again by the will of man but by the will of God! When I experience the new birth, I have begun the conforming process. I am being conformed to the image of God's Son.

One day Philip said to Jesus, " 'Show us the Father, and it is sufficient for us' " (John 14:8, *NKJV*). Jesus responded, " 'Have I been with you so long, and yet you have not known Me, Philip? He who has seen Me has seen the Father' " (v. 9, *NKJV*). He was telling us that He is the express image of the Godhead bodily. Jesus is the exact image of the Father. When you and I are conformed to His image, we will also look like our Father. His purpose is fulfilled, and we are fulfilled.

The controversy that served to obscure this wonderful truth began with the argument over whom God foreknew. The Scriptures have made it plain that God knows everything. He foretells the future because He foreknows it (Isaiah 46:10). Nothing is hidden from God. How ridiculous for man to presume that anyone has ever been born escaping the foreknowledge of God. He prescribed your parts before you were ever formed in the womb (Psalm 139:14-16). He foreknew you and everyone else.

Those He foreknew He also predestinated. Some have argued that every man is predestinated to either heaven or hell. But Paul said, rather, predestinated "to be conformed to the image of his Son."

Those He predestinated He also called. Who has God called? Scripture says He has called all men to repentance (Luke 24:47; 2 Peter 3:9). We are charged in the Great Commission to take the good news to every creature (Mark 16:15). Why should we take it to anyone whom God has left out? That would represent wasted effort on our part and an astounding cruelty on God's part.

"For . . . we both labour and suffer reproach, because we trust in the living God, who is the Saviour of all men, specially of those that believe" (1 Timothy 4:10). Paul declared that "God was in Christ, reconciling the [whole] world unto himself" (2 Corinthians 5:19). Yet it is necessary for me to believe. I must exercise my free will and choose to accept God's free gift. When I do, it becomes special to me. It was provided for everyone. Jesus died for the sins of the whole world. But it becomes personal and special to me when I commit myself to Him.

Some argue that because God is sovereign, His will cannot be thwarted. But His will is not thwarted. He exercised His sovereignty in giving me the opportunity to exercise my own will and in giving me room to do it. It is not God's will that any should perish. Yet men perish every day. God did not predestine them to perish. He predestined them all to be conformed to His image. He provided the opportunity in Christ. And He provides us the choice by His sovereign will.

At the instant of our new birth, we have the image of God restored to us. It is not mature. But it is present. Paul tells us in 2 Corinthians 3:18 that as we behold His face, we are changed into His image.

Likeness

God has said that He wants His family to be not only in His image but also after His likeness. Theologians could probably write great dissertations on image and likeness, but if we capture the ordinary meanings of these terms, we will be benefited a good deal.

When a baby is born into a home, it has image, but it does not have likeness. Most parents like to sleep all night. Most newborns don't. Most families like peace and quiet. Newborns don't give it a thought. Immediately the home is geared up to serve the baby's needs and to help it to develop likeness.

Jesus said to tell everybody the good news. Produce new births. Then He added, "Teaching them to observe all things whatsoever I have commanded you." Make disciples. What is that? It is to produce His likeness in His believers.

Process

Talking. Almost as soon as we have the new baby established on our daily schedule, we begin the effort to teach it how to say words. It requires hundreds of hours of speaking to the baby before it begins to return those words to us. After a while persistence pays off and it talks like us, including whatever accent the parents possess. The baby continues to enlarge its vocabulary for life. But it will speak like its parents most of the time.

In the same way, God has provided His Word for us. As we learn His Word, we can speak it back to Him. We can know when He speaks to us, for we know His words and His voice. The world will know we are of His family because we speak like Him. We enjoy His presence because we know Him and are becoming more like Him daily.

Walking. Soon after the baby learns some words, it also shows the desire to walk. It can crawl after a few months, but adults walk, so the baby desires to walk too. We spend hours helping it develop strength, balance and coordination for walking. Finally it happens. Now the child is more like its parents in the way it moves from place to place.

The Bible teaches us how to walk like our spiritual Father. The prophet asked the question, "Can two walk together, except they be agreed?" (Amos 3:3). As we learn to walk like God, we have the privilege of walking *with* Him.

Children eventually reach a level of maturity that qualifies them to run errands for the family. They walk and talk adequately for some responsibility. As we are faithful to learn God's talk and walk, He begins to send us on errands for Him.

Working. At about the age of 2 or 3, most parents begin to assign regular responsibility to each child. "Always pick up your toys." "Gather up the trash from all the trash cans and put it in the garbage can." Children help Mom with her work, and they like to help Dad with his. They are learning valuable lessons and learning how to be like their parents in attitude, outlook and performance. It is a valuable and precious experience.

The church is the family of God and is to provide every child of God the same kinds of opportunities (Ephesians 4).

Thus we work with our heavenly Father in the family of God and learn to be like Him. We begin to sense His presence in our service to Him.

Money. There comes a time when we decide to let each child receive an allowance or have an opportunity to work for money. Children must learn how to discipline themselves so they do not become wastrels or tightwads. It is far better that they learn the principles and make their mistakes with small amounts than to see them destroyed as adults.

We introduce them to planning, record keeping, tithing and sharing. As they accept our values and become dependable in carrying them out, we feel confident to trust them with more. The faithful child gets more privileges and matures much faster.

God also entrusts His children with certain resources. As we demonstrate an eagerness to be like Him, He can trust us with more. All of these growth experiences are for the fulfillment of God's original purpose that we develop after His likeness.

Every year we hear songs about there being no place like home for the holidays. We all know why. Home is where those people are who are most like us. Because of likeness we enjoy being together. We cherish it.

God wants likeness in us so we will enjoy spending time and eternity with Him. He has provided purpose, family, the Word and resources. He has given us stewardship of time, talent, testimony and treasure so that we may develop likeness. Jesus said, "It is enough for the disciple that he be as his master, and the servant as his lord" (Matthew 10:25).

David understood this purpose and testified, "I shall be satisfied when I awake in Your likeness (Psalm 17:15, *NKJV*).

John understood and wrote, "Now are we the sons of God . . . when he shall appear, we shall be like him; for we shall see him as he is" (1 John 3:2).

We see from the Scriptures then that God's original purpose for us is renewed in Christ. He restores image to us through the new birth. Likeness is developed through discipleship. Discipleship is the training program of God to enable us to be faithful stewards over all resources entrusted to us in this life. As God's stewards we exercise dominion. We participate in the operation of the kingdom of God.

Christ's example. Now we can see more clearly why God told Stanley Tam to give his business wholly to God. Jesus said, "Whosoever he be of you that forsaketh not all that he hath, he cannot be my disciple" (Luke 14:33). We cannot call Him Lord and hold back anything from Him. To be completely free men and women, we must place everything under His lordship and keep it there. To become conformed to Christ, we must follow His example by releasing everything to God.

Do you really want to be like Jesus? We sing songs declaring that we do, but do we really mean it? It requires giving everything to Him. We must let Him set us free from all selfishness. He is an unceasing giver. We must learn how to obey Him in giving if we are ever to be like Him.

Christ Our Example

Let's look at how much He gave and how freely He gave it. First, He gave up position so we could have a position of ruling and reigning. He gave up power as the Son of God; He emptied Himself so we could operate in the power of the Holy Spirit just as He did while on earth. He gave up His reputation as Creator to come and be our Savior. He gave up His riches so we could be made rich. In addition to that, He gave us His blood.

God declared that the penalty for sin was death. Since all have sinned and come short of the glory of God, all must die. The Old Testament tells us that the life is in the blood. Without the shedding of blood, there is no remission of sin. Yet if I shed my blood to settle this debt, I am left dead. Even then my sin debt is not paid because my blood is unacceptable . . . it was polluted by the same sin which created the debt. It can never pay the debt I owe God.

Jesus was begotten of the Father by the Holy Ghost. He was the second Adam. He never sinned. He did not have a sin nature. His blood was pure, and He came to give it for you and me.

After Jesus ministered for three and a half years, performing the greatest miracles ever seen by man, the time came for Him to give that perfect, sinless, redeeming blood for us. Have you ever stopped to consider the symbolism represented in each instance of His poured-out blood?

28

First blood. Actually, the first reference to the shedding of His blood was when He was only 8 days old—at circumcision. In that ceremony of dedication by his earthly parents, little baby Jesus gave some of that special blood. Remember Abraham and every male child of his for centuries entered into the covenant of promise through circumcision. But they were all sinners. Their blood was polluted by sin. God gave them covenant blessings on credit. Now Jesus' perfect blood paid for those centuries of covenant blessings.

Sanctified will. The next time we read of His blood being given was in the Garden of Gethsemane when He prayed that the Father would let the cup pass from Him. His sweat became as great drops of blood, and He proclaimed, "Not my will but thine be done."

Now look back to the first Adam and the Garden of Eden. There Adam essentially said to God, "Not Thy will but my will be done." Adam brought us into condemnation and turned man's will away from God.

Jesus literally sweat blood to provide the means whereby our will could be turned back to God. Now we can pray with power, "Not my will but Thy will be done." When you make that commitment, it is backed by the blood of Jesus.

Shamefaced. When the soldiers came to arrest Jesus, they pulled the hair from His face, as foretold by the prophet Isaiah (50:6). That special redeeming blood began to pour from the face of Jesus.

Remember when Adam sinned, he ran and hid. He could not face God, nor could we. The blood flowed from the face of Jesus to wash away the shame from our faces. Now we come boldly into the presence of God because of the amazing gift from our Lord Jesus Christ.

Blood and stripes. Next they beat His back, and that unique, unpolluted blood flowed copiously as they plowed His back and tore His flesh. Centuries before, when our forefathers first sinned, the burden of sickness and disease was placed upon the back of man. Here Jesus freely gave His blood and bore the stripes upon His back so that we could have the burden removed from our backs.

29

Crowning. Then they placed a crown of thorns upon His head, and the blood He had come to give flowed freely from the punctures in His brow. Adam had been crowned with dominion, but when he sinned, the crown fell. Now Jesus gave His precious blood through those wounds on His head so your head and mine can be sanctified to wear the crown again.

Hands. The time came to nail His hands to the cross. The blood flowed. After man sinned, he could not lift holy hands to worship God nor to serve God. As the blood flowed from the hands of Jesus, He provided cleansing for our hands. Now we can lift holy hands to worship Him and dedicate sanctified hands in service to Him.

Feet. Next they nailed His feet to the cross. His redeeming blood trickled down. You will remember that Adam's walks with God ceased after the rebellion. But now we walk with Him on a daily basis because of the gift of the blood of Jesus.

Open side. When Jesus died, there was still some blood left in His body. He had come to give all of it for you and me. A Roman soldier, with no idea of from where the impulse came to him, picked up a spear and thrust it into the side of our Savior. Blood and water gushed forth, showing that He was dead. His heart had burst within Him, He had given everything for us—especially His wonderful, redeeming, unpolluted blood.

You will recall that when Adam was alone in the Garden of Eden, God put him to sleep. After which, He opened up his side. He removed a rib and created a beautiful bride for Adam.

At Calvary the second Adam, God's only begotten Son, was put to sleep. His side was opened, and out of it came the purchase price of a bride for Jesus. The church was purchased that day so Jesus would not be God's only lonely Son. Because of the love of Jesus, His willingness to give everything—even His blood—God has that family He set out to produce in Genesis.

Do you really want to be like Jesus? Then you must become a giver. He gave all. And He is still giving. God is not selfish. When He only had one Son, He gave Him. Now He has millions of sons and daughters growing in His likeness through giving.

God is helping us to be like Jesus. He is teaching us to give. We are blessed . . . we have something to give . . . and opportunities to be a blessing.

CHAPTER 4

BLESSED WORSHIP

Two Ways to Worship

Cain and Abel came to worship (Genesis 4). Cain was a tiller of the soil. From the produce he had raised he brought an offering to the Lord. Abel was a keeper of livestock. He brought animal sacrifices to the Lord.

God refused Cain's offering. He accepted Abel's.

Some have suggested that Cain's offering was refused because it was not a blood sacrifice. A fairly good case can be made for that. Perhaps he should have traded with Abel or Adam and obtained some animals for worship.

Yet God accepted offerings from the field throughout the Old Testament. So there may be another problem here. Let's explore it.

The Septuagint translation renders God's statement to Cain, "Thou didst rightly present. Thou didst not rightly divide."

It appears that at least one of Cain's problems was he did not honor God with the first tenth. Cain had worked hard. Toiling by the sweat of his brow, he brought in a good crop. But 10 percent seemed far too much to give to God. God didn't really need it anyway. So he brought a nice-looking offering in the amount he decided was appropriate.

God refused it.

Abel brought the firstlings of his flock, which represented 10 percent or more. The very best was what Abel desired to give. He was not stingy with God.

God honored Abel for honoring Him. He accepted that which was presented joyfully and generously. Hebrews 11:4 says, "By faith Abel offered." In what was his faith placed? Did he depend on his animals for his survival, or did he believe God was His source?

Those questions were answered by the offerings, and so are ours. Abel's righteousness was revealed in his worship, in his faith, in his giving. Cain's sin was revealed in his worship, in his lack of faith, in his compromised giving. Stewardship reveals outwardly what is happening inwardly. Jesus said, "If you have not been faithful in the . . . unrighteous mammon . . . who will entrust to you the true riches?" (Luke 16:11, *Amp.*).

Cain discovered how quickly the attitude of irreverence toward God gets exposed. His irreverence indicates that he did not have proper regard for his brother nor proper esteem for himself. Cain passed over God's invitation to repent and take authority over the sin in his life. Instead of repenting and giving a blood sacrifice for his sin, Cain decided Abel was his problem. He sacrificed his brother's blood as the sin in his own heart came pouring out in action but not in repentance.

Righteous Abel was the victim of unrighteous Cain. The two families and their antagonized relationship are seen down through history. They are becoming very pronounced again as the world's hatred for the church rises up bolder and bolder each day.

Attitude Revealed

Our attitude toward God is clearly revealed in our attitude about our worship of Him in tithing and giving. A number of people within the church believe they can worship God in their "own way." However, that is dangerously close to, and can become, the way of Cain.

Where God has spoken in His Word concerning our approach to Him, we must diligently comply with that Word. We cannot add to nor subtract from what God has said. In the area of stewardship, which includes both worship and service, God has spoken clearly and copiously.

Coming to God "His way" is the religion of righteous Abel, who is listed in the faith Hall of Fame (Hebrews 11) for his great faith evidenced by his correct giving. Yes, he did suffer persecution. He was killed for his righteousness. The alternative is to go the way of Cain. He lived the rest of his life in shame under God's judgment and is remembered for his bad example.

Apparently, Abel understood. God owns it all. I am His steward. I am to worship with a generous, cheerful heart. I will withhold nothing from God. He is my source and my security. Cain thought those possessions were his. He was willing to worship but on his own terms. Like his parents, he failed in his stewardship. That failure led to other sins and to a pitiful and tragic life. They are powerful examples to you and me.

Blessed to Be a Blessing

God chose a man named Abraham to be the father of the faithful. This man had a unique and wonderful relationship with God. Abraham was exceptional in many ways. But he was still a man. Nevertheless, God used him as a patriarch, an example and a steward.

In Genesis 12 God told Abraham to get out of his country, leave his kindred, his father's house, and go to a land that God would show him. He was promised some important blessings for his obedience. God said, "I will make of thee a great nation, and I will bless thee, and make thy name great; and thou shalt be a blessing" (v. 2).

It cost Abraham something to obey. The terms were that he would father a great nation, but not in his own country. He would become a foreigner in another land. God promised to bless him, but not among his own kinsmen. He had to leave them. God was going to make his name great, but not in his father's house. God's blessing was not just to Abraham, it was to also flow through him as a means of blessing others.

If Abraham had not been obedient to God's instruction, we would never have heard of him. But there is no contemporary of Abraham's whose name is so well-known through all generations, including our own. Secular history rarely, if ever, mentions Abraham. Yet God made his name great and keeps it great with no help from the historians.

Consider one other key ingredient in Abraham's experience. He built altars wherever he went. Altars to facilitate his worship and his giving represented the importance Abraham placed upon his relationship with God. The two exceptions to Abraham's practice of building altars and worshiping wherever he went occurred in Egypt and Gerar. It is significant that those are the two places where he was separated from his wife. Except for God's intervention, he would have lost her in either place.

The principle of blessing is still in effect. God desires to bless us and make us a blessing to others. He still requires obedience. We must be willing to give up our own country, kinsmen and our father's house if God asks for that. He wants us to look to Him as our source, not to our own resources, friends, influence or family.

He also wants us to build our relationship with Him and always keep it first. If we build altars unto Him everywhere we go, then we will see His protection upon our family. Should we forget this priority, we run a great risk that our family will become one of the sad statistics of broken homes.

While the national tragedy of divorce claims nearly half the marriages in America, some are marvelously protected. One study indicates that the couples who pray together daily see only one breakup per 11,000 marriages. Those family altars were important for Abraham and they are important for us.

The Holy Spirit revealed to my wife during a time of study how the principle of "blessed to be a blessing" is presented in the New Testament. "As every man hath received the gift, even so minister the same one to another, as good stewards of the manifold grace of God" (1 Peter 4:10).

When we responded to God's invitation to be born again, He gave us saving grace. And He made us a steward of saving grace so that every time we encounter someone who needs to be born again, we can share saving grace with him.

If we have experienced divine healing, then we received God's healing grace. Since that time we have been a steward of healing grace so that we can share it with others who need to be healed. Each time God answers a prayer for us, it is by His grace. Each time our stewardship of grace is enlarged to make us a source to others. We are blessed to be a blessing.

The apostle Paul said, "Blessed be God, even the Father of our Lord Jesus Christ, the Father of mercies, and the God of all comfort; who comforteth us in all our tribulation, that we may be able to comfort them which are in any trouble, by the comfort wherewith we ourselves are comforted of God" (2 Corinthians 1:3, 4). This New Testament teaching will be apparent throughout our study of the principles of stewardship.

God is the source of all blessing. We are His stewards as well as His children. He blesses us on the basis of this relationship and our faithfulness to His instruction. And then He uses us to channel His blessings to others. Abraham gave us a powerful example.

Understanding the Blessing Principle

Abraham not only illustrated the gospel principle of "blessed to be a blessing," but his life proved that he had real understanding in the whole area of stewardship.

There was strife between the herdsmen of Abraham's cattle and the herdsmen of Lot's cattle. Because their substance was so great, they could no longer dwell together. Abraham confronted the problem. He spoke to Lot of his desire for peace.

Abraham had received the promise from God that this land was for his own heirs through a promised son not yet received (Genesis 12:7). In spite of that promise, he offered Lot first choice of the land. Lot chose the grassy, well-watered plains to the east . . . an obviously wise choice economically.

Abraham held no resentment at all toward Lot for taking advantage of his generosity. He understood that his security was not to be found in grass but in his relationship with the true and living God. Abraham demonstrated that if we will sincerely prefer our brother, then we may reliably expect God to be our source. And he was never confused concerning this basic truth as to his source of supply. He never thought that creation was the origin of his blessing. He looked to his Creator in faith.

Immediately following Lot's departure, God promptly confirmed his promise to Abraham of all the land he could see, including that which he had graciously shared with Lot. God commanded him not only to see the land but to walk through it, "for I will give it unto thee." Abraham moved to the plain of Mamre in Hebron, and there he built an altar (Genesis 13:14-18). Lot soon discovered that the choice he had made led him closer and closer to the city of Sodom, a wicked city. Before long he moved inside the walls. God's blessing upon his life gave him prominence. His spiritual standing with God was a witness to the people of that city.

Besides the exceeding wickedness of Sodom, they also had to pay high taxes. Chedorlaomer was a powerful king in the region who exacted heavy tribute from all the cities. His taxation was enforced through an alliance he had forged with three other kings who also had substantial armies.

After 12 years of high taxes, the cities rebelled. Chedorlaomer responded by bringing his armies. He defeated the armies of the subject cities. He took everything of value. And he took hostages. Lot and his family were carried away captive.

One young man escaped the marauding soldiers. He hurried to the hill country to give the bad news to Abraham. Abraham's response was quick and decisive. He called for all of the male servants born in his own house to stand forth, receive their swords and follow him in pursuit of this enemy's armies.

We have to be impressed with Abraham's faith. Can you imagine the audacity? One rancher and 318 cowhands going after four professional, victorious armies.

Of course, Abraham did have faith. He is the father of the faithful. He had such a relationship with God that he believed God not only could fulfill every promise but that He would. His faith was strong enough to set him free. He was free from the paralysis of fear. He was free from the frustration of indecision. He was free to do what righteousness called for in the face of overwhelming circumstances. He was free to fight evil. He enjoyed the freedom of true faith in the true God and in God's every word.

You and I can have that same freedom through our relationship with God. When we devote as much time and thought to the words of God each day, when we establish an altar of worship and live our lives around that altar, then we will experience the Abraham kind of faith. When we give ourselves fully to God, then we will not fear man or circumstance.

The question is often asked, Why does the church have so little impact on the world today? The answer can be drawn from Abraham's example.

Too much of the time God's Word is debated instead of believed. We are found arguing instead of obeying. Not only do Christians fail to establish altars in their homes, many churches no longer have altars. Power departed the church when prevailing prayer was deleted. Spiritual power is absent in every home where altars of devotion are absent.

We do not have to wait for everybody else, however. Abraham stood alone much of the time. A part of the legacy we receive from him is the example of being first in spiritual matters. God will grant relationship to us when we pay the price. He said we would find Him when we seek Him with all of our heart (Deuteronomy 4:29-31).

Can you imagine the conversation among Abraham's servants when he told them they were going after Chedorlaomer?

"We're going after four armies? We don't have one army!"

"They're professional soldiers; we are herdsmen."

"They're veterans. Look what they did to all the armies of the plains. We are inexperienced at this sort of thing."

"Well, yes, Abraham gave us swords, but we're amateurs."

They probably felt somewhat like the young man visiting the rodeo. When he was unexpectedly seated on a Brahma bull, he lamented, "I ain't' no cowboy. I just found this hat."

39

The men in Abraham's impromptu herdsmen army surely experienced some consternation. But remember, they were all born in Abraham's house. They had been witnesses to his faith and worship all of their lives. They had heard him speak of the faithfulness of God. And they had observed God's provision and protection upon him and upon them. Abraham was God's proof of His power and truthfulness.

These herdsmen may not have been ready for war through military training and experience, but they were well-prepared spiritually. They had been in God's school of faith for many years.

God wants us to be ready for every situation in life too. The preparation comes daily as we fellowship with Him in worship—the altar; as we listen to and learn His Word—the school; and as we live out His principles in each situation—the proof. Yes, we are God's proof (Romans 12:2). By our faithfulness to God we prove to the world that the Bible is true. As we obey the principles of stewardship, our life illustrates how powerful they are. We are God's proof to a wicked and gainsaying world. We are blessed to be a blessing.

Abraham not only overtook Chedorlaomer, he not only engaged him in battle, he not only defeated him, he and his impromptu army slaughtered those hardened veterans. They rescued the hostages and recovered all the wealth that had been taken from the cities of the plains.

Abraham returned with one of the greatest military victories of all time. He didn't lose one man. This is like David's killing of Goliath. It is comparable to Israel's Six-Day War. He demonstrated the mighty power of God to a skeptical world . . . and to us. Meditate upon this true story. Understand it. See how your faith will increase.

God shows no partiality. He will give each of us the same kind of faith. He will give us the same kind of victory in our life. Every challenge we face is an opportunity for God to receive glory—by bringing us through it with great victory. The principles Abraham lived by are based upon truth. They still work, and they will work for each of us.

LOOK AT THE PRINCIPLES

Celebrating Victory

Upon his return from the slaughter of Chedorlaomer and the kings who were with him, Abraham entered into one of the most powerful teaching examples of his life. Some profound symbols are used in the biblical account of this incident to enlarge our understanding.

First, Abraham encountered the King of Sodom. This man ruled over a city that God would judge and destroy in a few short years. The city was so overrun with homosexuality that its name, Sodom, is still used to describe homosexuals—Sodomites, and their perverted practices—sodomy. This man—King Bera—is an apt spokesman for the spirit entity named Satan.

When Abraham encountered Bera, you can be sure this king had nice things to say. He was full of congratulations and compliments because he understood the magnitude of Abraham's exploits as well as anyone could. After all, he had been totally humiliated by Chedorlaomer and only escaped by running to the slime pits and falling in. Perhaps his escape had succeeded because once he was in the slime, the conquering soldiers didn't feel he was worth their getting filthy just to capture or kill him. He was truly grateful to Abraham for avenging him and vanquishing such a formidable enemy.

Despite the king's greeting and kind words, a strange thing occurred. Abraham, a gracious man at all times, would not be engaged in conversation. He refused to be delayed. He very deliberately proceeded to his destination. His mission was not yet fully completed. Abraham was on his way to worship. He and his little army were going to church.

Rest and Works

Abraham illustrated for us the Sunday principle. He understood that his great victory was not of his own making. The true and living God whom he served had protected his life and guided his strategy. Now he would lead his men to worship their great benefactor and give thanks.

God had set an example in Creation by working six days and then resting on the seventh. All through the Old Testament the Jews honored this pattern. They worked all week to earn a day of rest and worship on Saturday. They were recognizing by this practice that God is Creator.

In the New Testament we take our day of rest and worship on the first day of the week—the Lord's Day. We begin at rest and the works follow. Why? Because Jesus already did the work for us. We have ceased from our own labors and entered into His rest (see Hebrews 4:9, 10). Just as Old Testament believers honored God as Creator by seventh-day rest and worship, we honor Him as redeemer through first-day rest and worship. The old-covenant believer worked hard, looking forward to a day of rest. But we begin at rest, and the works we do are simply the fruit of our relationship with Him.

Abraham was the best one to illustrate this principle. He was the father of God's chosen people, the Jews. And he is the father of the New Testament family of the faithful (Galatians 3:29).

We celebrate our redemption through Jesus Christ every Lord's Day. It is a constant reminder that He is to be first in every part of our lives. He is to have preeminence in my life as He did in Abraham's life.

Bera, king of Sodom, would have delayed Abraham on his way to worship even though his motives appeared in order. What harm could come from it? Much. Abraham was unwilling to receive the accolades of the world, or conduct business, until his worship experience and time of thanksgiving prepared his heart.

We would do well to remember that there is a weakness in the heart of man that is easily exploited after great success. King Bera would not have been disposed to acknowledge God's part in Abraham's victory. He would have exalted Abraham. He would have lauded man's great ability. He would have appealed to human pride. If pride had been aroused in Abraham's heart, then God would have resisted him (see 1 Peter 5:5). Abraham would no longer have been God's free man, but he would have fallen into bondage. That's one of the reasons he had such determination to go on to church where they could celebrate the One who gave the victory and keep a correct perspective of life.

The enemy of your soul has a plan for dealing with you during the vulnerable time of great success. The world will applaud you—but not the God you serve. If you accept the applause, if you receive glory unto yourself, then your journey to God's house will be interrupted. You will discover that success brings a cruel bondage if it is not immediately subordinated to the lordship of Christ. Many have learned that success in business, academics, sports or the arts first interrupted the church priority and then destroyed their personal relationship with God. "God resisteth the proud, but He giveth grace unto the humble" (James 4:6).

King Without Beginning

The second king Abraham encountered upon his return was a most unusual person. He had an interesting name—Melchizedek. His title was king of Salem. Many believe he was king of the city we call Jerusalem.

Just as King Bera had adequate qualifications to identify him as symbolic spokesman for Satan, King Melchizedek has profound qualifications as symbolic spokesman for Jesus

Christ. First, the name of his kingdom means peace. Jesus is the Prince of Peace. At His birth the angels sang, "Peace on earth." During His ministry He taught, "My peace I give unto you." Under His millennial reign we will have worldwide peace for the first time since Adam's fall.

Jews, Christians and Arabs look to Jerusalem as a city of paramount importance to their faith. Jerusalem was high in elevation. Sodom was below sea level. Jerusalem is known for its influence to lift men. Sodom is known for its influence to pull them down. Jerusalem will be the world's capital in the future. Sodom is already judged and destroyed. The city God has prepared to rule the universe is named New Jerusalem. Jesus is the king of New Jerusalem. His spokesman in Genesis 14 was king of Salem.

Melchizedek didn't have a father or a mother (Hebrews 7:3). The first couple, Adam and Eve, were the only other people who didn't have earthly parents. They were created children of God. The second Adam, Jesus Christ, did have a mother in the sense that Mary furnished him a body. But we know Jesus was Himself the preexistent Creator (John 1:1-3). Mary provided Him a body for His earthly mission, but in light of His eternal existence, He had no parents. This is another similarity between Christ and Melchizedek.

Scripture also declares of this unusual person that he was "without descent" (Hebrews 7:3). Obviously, if he did not have a father or mother, neither would he have lineage. Scripture traces the family tree of Mary in her role as provider of Christ's body. Yet, since no one preceded Him in eternity, He has no lineage or descent in the eternal sense.

Another strange fact about Melchizedek was that he had "neither beginning of days, nor end of life" (Hebrews 7:3). Neither did Jesus have a beginning of days. He was Himself the beginner of days (Colossians 1:16).

The priestly parallel is extremely important. "For this Melchisedec, king of Salem, priest of the most high God, who met Abraham returning from the slaughter of the kings, and blessed him" (Hebrews 7:1). Melchizedek was both king and priest. Jesus fills both positions too. Revelation 19:16 calls

Him "King of Kings." Hebrews 3:1 calls Him the "High Priest of our profession." Melchizedek was "King of righteousness" (Hebrews 7:2). Jesus is made unto us righteousness (1 Corinthians 1:30). And Revelation 19:11 says, "In righteousness he doth judge and make war."

This parallel is important to our understanding of stewardship. That's why we are given this particular information in Scripture. Remember how Melchizedek's and Christ's roles parallel. Both are kings and priests. They are kings of peace and righteousness and of Jerusalem—Melchizedek of earthly Jerusalem and Christ of New Jerusalem. They are priests forever and of the same order or rank, which means they are both high priests. They have no beginning and no end, no forefathers or natural descendants; and they both receive tithes (Genesis 14:20; Hebrews 7:8). There is yet another profound parallel as we shall see.

Some Bible scholars even suggest that Melchizedek actually constituted an Old Testament appearance of Jesus. A very strong case can be made for that argument. However, we can establish the understanding we need simply by recognizing that Melchizedek certainly spoke for Jesus and represented Him whether or not he was actually Jesus.

Communion

Abraham came to where Melchizedek was and they had a worship service. Evidently, all of Abraham's servants were still with him. He certainly could not transport the wealth of the cities of the plains without help. We can reasonably believe that the congregation consisted of Abraham, his 318 servants (perhaps some of their families had joined them as well), and the king of Sodom as observer.

Melchizedek brought forth bread and wine. He served Communion. We tend to think of the serving of bread and wine as a New Testament sacrament, and it is. But the Jews had observed it in Passover for centuries, anticipating the coming Messiah. Melchizedek's serving preceded the first Passover by more than 400 years. He served Communion the way Christ would to His disciples in Matthew 26:26.

45

Why did Melchizedek serve Communion to Abraham? We must answer that question to have a proper understanding of the tithe.

The apostle Paul tells us in Galatians 3:8 that God preached the gospel to Abraham. What is the gospel? The good news of Jesus Christ exclusively. God shared it with Abraham in Genesis 12:1-3. What was Abraham's response?

Abraham believed the gospel. And "it was imputed to him for righteousness" (Romans 4:22; see also Galatians 3:6). How does God impute righteousness to us? Only in response to our faith in Jesus Christ. It was the same for Abraham. So Abraham was a believer in the same Jesus in whom we believe. Abraham believed before Jesus' visit to Calvary. We believe after Calvary. Abraham was just as qualified to receive Christian Communion as you or I or any other Christian. Therefore, Melchizedek served him.

Following the serving of Communion, Melchizedek then blessed Abraham by sharing God's words of love and God's intention for Abraham to be fulfilled and happy. He reminded Abraham that this blessing was from the Most High God who is possessor of heaven and earth. That is a foundational truth—God is owner of everything. Melchizedek declared it. Abraham believed it.

The next part of the worship service is probably where Abraham raised his hands (Genesis 14:22). In this part of the worship, they blessed God. They gave God praise and expressed their love to Him. They also acknowledged that Abraham's great military victory was the gift of God to Abraham.

The final part of the worship was when Abraham presented tithes. He gave the first tenth of all the transportable wealth from the cities of the plains. At this point Abraham was giving concrete evidence that all the things he had said about God were true. His actions now demonstrated his testimony. He honored the Lord with his substance and with the firstfruits of all his increase (Proverbs 3:9).

Some interesting questions arise concerning this act of

tithing by Abraham. Why did he pay tithes on that which he had possessed for only a few hours and which he intended to give back to its original owners? Because Abraham understood that when he received an increase of possessions, they must be deliberately brought under the lordship of God.

Adam had been granted trusteeship over the earth. When he acted upon Satan's word, he forfeited his trusteeship to Satan. Satan referred to this transfer in his temptation of Christ (Luke 4:6). Satan is not the owner. God has always been owner and always will be. But man's fall yielded that which had been entrusted to man over to our enemy temporarily. The Enemy religiously uses those possessions to tempt man. He knows if he can produce covetousness in the heart of man, he will have led him into idolatry. Ultimately, all idolatry is devil worship. Satan's ploy to use material things in his effort to induce Christ to worship him didn't work. But it works in the lives of millions of people every day.

The reason the Bible contains over 700 verses dealing with money and possessions is that Satan has had such great success in destroying man through this means. God provided the power to defeat this weakness. Abraham had this power of God at work in his life through a profound practice the Bible calls tithing.

Modern man has an ancient dilemma. We are in a material world. We use things for our physical needs. Money is a convenient medium of exchange. The world, the flesh and the devil all tempt us to take security in things. But if we do, we have become idolaters. We have yielded to worshiping and serving the creation instead of the Creator. We have become entrapped in the error of our foreparents Adam and Eve.

Jesus taught copiously on this ever-present threat. He referred to material possessions as "unrighteous mammon," and Paul called money "filthy lucre." Believers are taught to put away all filthiness. Yet we carry money with us most of the time. We are told to forsake all unrighteousness. Yet we own material possessions and keep money deposited in the bank under our name. How can we reconcile this dilemma? How can we be faithful children of God living in a world where we use so much that is under the influence of the god of this world?

The apostle Paul gave the answer in Romans 11:16. He said that "if the firstfruit be holy, the lump is also holy." Praise the Lord! I don't have to be in possession of filthy lucre or unrighteous mammon. Each time God increases my trusteeship of the things of this world, I can immediately sanctify that increase by tithing it.

If I fail to tithe it, then I have in my possession property upon which Satan has a legitimate claim. I give him the opportunity he seeks to influence and to pull me back under his control through possessions.

I have been unable to find any other practice in the Old or New Testaments which offers the opportunity to break the power of possessions to be used against us. Tithing is the ancient principle God has given to His people that enables us to cope with one of the most pervasive threats to our spirituality. That is not to say the believer cannot misuse possessions that have been tithed. It happens all too often. Yet the authority of Satan over possessions entrusted to us is broken by the tithe. We are then free to use those possessions to the glory of God.

Abraham understood this powerful principle. That's why he tithed that which he intended to give away. Abraham was unwilling to own anything for even a few hours without dedicating it to God.

Another important aspect of Abraham's tithing is that he paid tithes to Melchizedek, the Old Testament's best representative of Jesus Christ. The tithe has always been to Christ. This particular incident was used by the Holy Spirit for teaching the principles involved in tithing, not because it was the first time anyone had tithed but because it so powerfully represented tithing to Christ. Interestingly, Melchizedek was used to present the first teaching on tithing in the Old Testament and the last teaching on tithing in the New Testament.

CHAPTER 6

GOD'S ILLUSTRATIONS

The Feasts of Jehovah

God gives us teachings in the Holy Scripture. He also provides illustrations to assist our learning of His teachings. The seven feasts of Jehovah are presented to us in Leviticus 23. Each one of them is an illustration of the ministry of Jesus to us. Much of the truth concerning Jesus was enfolded in these illustrations and would not be unfolded until Jesus came. The Jews observed the feasts every year. They understood some of what was being presented, but as the years passed, they seemed to get further from the essential truth. By the time Jesus came, He referred to the feasts as the feasts of the Jews rather than feasts of Jehovah. They had drifted that far from the original understanding God had purposed to share with them.

Passover. The first feast was the Passover. This annual dramatization of the ministry of Jesus in salvation is the feast most often learned by Christians. Yet we have missed much of the richness of this illustration through our failure to explore it thoroughly enough. How many Christian men see the high calling and privilege extended to them through this feast?

The first priest in the feast of the Passover was the father of each family. He slew the lamb, placed the blood on the doorpost of their home, presented the sacrifice to his family, and taught them its meaning. God still calls each man to be the priest of his home; to present Christ, the Lamb of God, to his family, to inculcate in them the understanding of the sacrifice and the blood; and to minister salvation to them.

Unleavened Bread. The second feast was the Feast of Unleavened Bread. Here we have the revelation of Christ's ministry of sanctification to us—His power to defeat sin in our lives. He is the bread of life, that unleavened manna sent down from heaven. By the power of His life we may rid our lives of the sin, or leaven, which is so generally prevalent.

Again the priest in this feast was the man of the house. He received significant participation from his wife in both of these feasts. The mother would do spring housecleaning in anticipation of these feasts. She would remove from her home all leaven and everything made from leaven. Finally, she would pitch a small amount of leaven, reserved for this special purpose, into a corner somewhere in her home.

The father would then go with the children to search for the leaven remaining in their home. Dad would carry a lighted candle and a feather. The children would be delighted when they found the leaven. Then Dad would sweep it up with the feather and cast it out of the house.

The mother had the leaven at one time. Why didn't she throw it out? For a very good reason. Although Mom works constantly to keep sin out of the home, Dad is still the priest of the home. It is his responsibility to keep sin out and to teach the children how to identify sin and dispose of it.

The lighted candle represents the Word of God. "Thy word is a lamp unto my feet" (Psalm 119:105). The feather is a symbol of the Holy Spirit (Mark 1:10). We can only find sin in our homes or our lives by the light of the Word. The world constantly changes the names of sin in an effort to hide it. The world calls the sin of sodomy, homosexuality, an alternate lifestyle. The world calls the sin of drunkenness, alcoholism, a disease. The Bible does not call for sympathy for sin, but it calls for repentance of these and all other sins.

Only by the light of the Word can we locate and identify sin. Only by the help of the Holy Spirit can we sweep it out of our lives.

Firstfruits. The third feast of Jehovah is the Feast of Firstfruits. In the observance of this feast, we see a dramatization of the power of Christ in the management of material possessions. Even though I committed my life to Jesus at a certain point in my life, and at that time I confessed His lordship over me and everything entrusted to me, I have constantly received additions to my trusteeship since that time. They need to be dedicated to my Lord also.

Just as in the other feasts, the Jewish procedure for observing this feast has many symbols and is highly instructive. At planting time for the winter barley, the priest would place three hoops on the ground in a freshly sown field. As the barley grew, the hoops would no longer be visible. But the priest had to remember where they were placed because he had to come back later to retrieve them.

The Feast of Firstfruits occured each year just as the barley reached maturity. The priest who placed the hoops in the field now returned. He brought another priest with him and some witnesses. One of them knelt down to cut the barley that had grown inside the first hoop. Three times he asked if the sun was yet down and waited for a confirming word from the one who was standing. The one standing was watching and waiting for the sun to be fully down. When the sun was completely below the horizon, he gave the word to cut the barley. They quickly cut all that had grown inside the three hoops and headed back to the Temple.

The next morning was the time for a most meaningful worship service. Farmers brought bundles of their firstfruits from their fields and gathered to participate in this significant event. The priest offered a lamb for a burnt offering. He offered a "meat-offering" of fine flour and oil for a sweet smelling savor to God (Leviticus 23:13). He presented the special bundle of firstfruits in a wave offering and then poured out a wine offering before the Lord. Finally, when the ceremony was completed, according to *Pulpit Commentary*, the priest went before the gathered people to give a momentous announcement. "Now the firstfruits have been sanctified holy unto the Lord. Now the whole harvest is sanctified holy unto Him. You may go and harvest your fields."

Each of the feasts is rich in symbolism and provides a tremendous dramatization of different aspects of the ministry of Jesus Christ. The symbols are profound in the richness with which they represent insight and understanding of the work of our Lord Jesus in our behalf. Paul spoke of the satisfaction available to us in the revelation of Christ: "In whom [Christ] are hid all the treasures of wisdom and knowledge" (Colossians 2:3). Christ referred to this same insight when He proclaimed, "Search the scriptures; for in them ye think ye have eternal life: and they are they which testify of me" (John 5:39).

We need an understanding of these symbols to better comprehend Christ our Lord so that we may, in turn, become accomplished stewards of all He has entrusted to us.

When the Jewish priest entered into the freshly sown field of barley to mark the special bundles that would be harvested for the firstfruits ceremony, he did not recognize the greatest significance of their number. He was quite unaware of the triune God. Yet his three hoops were apt symbols of Father, Son and Holy Spirit. They are each self-existent. They have no beginning and no end. Hence, a circle is an appropriate symbol of their eternity—endlessness.

The three rings in the field also spoke of God's sovereign power to originate. Not only did He create all that is, but it is only by His power that there can be any increase. The farmers prepared the soil God had created and, with the strength and skill He shared with them, worked by the light of the sun given by God, planted seed only He can supply, and waited for rain which He delivered. As the barley grew, those three circular markers were testifying that God is in the increase.

All blessing is from God. "Every good gift and every perfect gift is from above, and cometh down from the Father"

(James 1:17). You have never received a blessing except from Him. He is the source. He is the supply. You will never receive a blessing from any other source. The three rings in the barley field testified that God is in the increase. Unless we acknowledge this truth we are held in darkness, unable to adequately relate to Him or His creation.

When the priests returned to harvest the special first-fruits, they were celebrating in advance our Lord's sacrifice at Calvary. Upon receiving a positive answer to his query regarding the sunset, he would then wield the blade and cut the three shocks of barley. The witnesses looked on to see what was done and to see that the integrity of the procedures was not compromised.

Years later Christ grew up among men as one specially marked to represent the Trinity. He was brought before the priest and accused. But no disqualifying fault was ever found in Him. When it was time for Him to be cut down, His life had already borne testimony that God is the only source of salvation. There is no other. There can be no other.

God turned off the lights on the face of the whole earth that afternoon when Christ hung on the cross. It was a testimony to the necessary reality that Christ had volunteered to submit to the power of darkness as a means of breaking its power (Luke 22:53). It revealed one of the reasons the priest always waited for the sunset before cutting down the first-fruits of barley. They were illustrating that Christ would not be harvested in the light of day.

Another reason for the delay until sunset was that the Jewish day began at sunset. The priests entered the barley field at the end of the Sabbath. When the sun was fully set, it was Sunday—the Lord's Day. The earth was overwhelmed by darkness, both physical and spiritual, when Christ died. But on Sunday the Lord was victor! Darkness was forever defeated! The Feast of Firstfruits was a Sunday feast. It was to be celebrated on the Lord's Day. It has always been for Jesus. He is Himself firstfruits (1 Corinthians 15:23). And firstfruits offerings are for Him.

Back at the Temple the priest offered a sacrifice of a lamb for a burnt offering. Jesus was the Lamb of God slain from the foundation of the world (Revelation 13:8). He not only died to save us but also to give the power necessary to keep us in a world of unrighteousness. We would not survive in our walk with the Lord as we handle filthy lucre and unrighteous mammon without the power granted through His sacrifice and His procedure detailed in His Word.

The next offering was fine flour mingled with oil, an offering made by fire to the Lord for a sweet savor. Our Lord Jesus was the bread come down from heaven, unleavened bread, as a revelation from God to us and as a sacrifice to God for us. He was as fine flour (uncontaminated by sin) mixed with the oil of the Holy Spirit. His life and sacrifice did present a sweet savor to the Father.

Jesus is the Word (John 1:14). Jesus, the Word, is bread to us (John 6:35). The Holy Spirit is symbolized by oil. He was sent to guide us into all truth (John 16:13). When we receive the bread of the Word, understand it by the oil of the Holy Spirit and obey it in our living, then our lives are also a sweet-smelling sacrifice to God. The world will provide the fire of persecution (see Matthew 13:21) because of the Word in our lives and our commitment to it. But they are helping us to fulfill God's purpose in us through their resistance to us.

A wine offering was also a part of the Feast of Firstfruits. Clearly the wine represents the blood of Jesus. Blood flows through a body to wash away the wastes and to bring nourishment. Jesus' blood flows through the body of Christ and cleanses us of all sin. His blood gives us the nourishment of His very life. Without that cleansing flow we would die from the contamination of living in a fallen world and handling unrighteous mammon.

A special part of this ceremony was the wave offering of the three-parts sheaf cut for presenting to God as firstfruits. The priest waved the sheaf up and down vertically, then horizontally. He followed the pattern of the cross hundreds of years before the Romans introduced the cruel practice of crucifying condemned men on crosses. Clearly the priest was typifying the greatest event of history when Jesus Christ would be a wave offering suspended between heaven and earth. He was God's firstfruits given to us. Yet He was also the firstfruits of men given as an offering to God.

When the priest had completed all of the ceremony of the firstfruits feast, he was ready for an announcement to all the worshipers. "Now the firstfruits have been sanctified holy unto God. Now the whole harvest is sanctified and holy unto Him. You may go and harvest your crops."

Jesus made a similar announcement to His disciples after He had been offered up. Just before He ascended back to heaven to reclaim His throne, He declared, "Go ye into all the world, and preach the gospel to every creature"—that is, make converts of all nations. Do you see the similarity in the priest's announcement concerning barley harvest and Christ's commission to the spiritual harvest?

There is still a vital parallel to be observed here. We must not miss the power and purpose in the Feast of Firstfruits to sanctify material possessions. The dedication of the firstfruits was a pledge. In bringing the firstfruits, the worshiper was declaring God's ownership over all of the increase. He was committed to bring the tithe promptly upon harvesting his fields. He would be a robber of God if he did not bring the tithes. Without this pledge his crop would not be sanctified and could bring evil to him instead of blessing (Malachi 3:9). To consume one grain of a new crop before sanctifying the firstfruits would mean that he would be cut off from Israel and Israel's God through disobedience.

In the New Testament we begin our walk with the Lord by first proclaiming His lordship—ownership over everything (Romans 10:9). We are admitting the same truth as the worshiper in the Feast of Firstfruits. And just like them, we have continued to receive regular increases from the Lord. How will we sanctify these material blessings unto Him and maintain our profession that He is Lord of everything?

The firstfruits principle is in operation forever (Leviticus 23:10, 14). As long as we deal with material things, we will show forth the lordship of Christ over all that is under our trusteeship. It is more important now than in the future, however, because now we are redeemed people living in a fallen world. We are subject to, and must be vigilant against, being drawn back into sin and death through covetousness or disobedience. We are a message to the lost.

There is only one way to sanctify that increase which comes to us out of this sinful world. We can apply the firstfruits principle to it. Paul reminded us of it in Romans 11:16: "If the firstfruit be holy, the lump is also holy." We can bring all that is under our control under the lordship of Jesus through the tithe. This sanctifying of possessions through firstfruits and tithes is well illustrated in Leviticus 27.

Firstfruits are to remind us of God's ownership by virtue of His act of creation. It was on the first day of Creation that the Holy Spirit moved on earth's chaos to bring order. And on the first day God shined forth light and separated the light from the darkness.

We invoke the movement of the Holy Spirit upon our own financial chaos when we tithe. By this act we also proclaim the lordship of Jesus Christ. He is the Light. Thereby he shines into the darkness of our worldly stewardship and permits us to see the proper order. He even separates that which has been sanctified to Him from that which is still under the control of the world, just as He separated light from darkness.

Three Empty Places

One other point we need to consider before we leave firstfruits is given to us in the field where the priest cut three portions of firstfruits. He put the three portions into one bundle, which resembles Christ, the express image of the Godhead bodily. He is three in one.

Even the empty places of the field communicate a message. Christ the firstfruits (1 Corinthians 15:23) also left three empty places in order to bring salvation to us.

The throne. The first empty place reminds us that Christ

sat upon a throne beside His Father from before time began. They had constant uninterrupted fellowship until the Father declared it was time for Christ to come to earth and take on the form of man.

For nine months He was carried in the womb of Mary. The throne upon which He had sat for millennia was now empty. Angels had worshiped Him ceaselessly. Now they observed an empty place beside the Father. Heaven had given up its greatest delight.

When Mary and Joseph went to Bethlehem, it was time for the birth of Jesus. The night He was delivered, the angels came pouring out of heaven. They had come to celebrate . . . to worship Him!

Shepherds saw the most amazing sight. Worship that had heretofore taken place in heaven around the throne was now visible to them . . . around a stable. They were invited to join in. They did.

But the throne was still empty. For more than 34 years Christ voluntarily gave up His throne for us. Heaven sacrificed its awesome Son and stared at the empty place—part of the price that must be paid for us.

The cross. The second empty place in the barley field reminds us of another empty place in the life of Jesus. Some religious beliefs show the symbol of the cross with Jesus still on the cross. Most Protestant faiths display an empty cross. We know He has already been there and completed the work of Calvary. He returned to His throne, but He will never return to the cross.

God declared that the penalty for sin was death. The life is in the blood. "Without shedding of blood is no remission" (Hebrews 9:22). "All have sinned, and come short of the glory of God" (Romans 3:23). Because of my sin, I was under the sentence of death. My sin had polluted my blood, and it could not therefore pay the moral debt incurred by my sin. Only perfect blood of a sinless individual could meet the demands of God's justice. That perfect blood existed only in One begotten of God himself. He had to be conceived by a virgin who was overshadowed by the Holy Spirit. That only begotten Son had to live a sinless life. And then He had to die for you ... and me.

Jesus volunteered for the mission. He gave up everything for us. And then He gave Himself. It was necessary that Jesus volunteer for the cross. They could not take Him otherwise. The arresting soldiers fell down when He told them who He was. Had He spoken in His defense, the judges would have fallen too.

That cross was waiting for us. We sinned. We were under sentence of death. Jesus took our place. His body was emptied of that perfect blood. Our debt was paid. But it cost Him everything to set us free. Don't ever forget that empty cross. It was part of the price of our salvation.

The tomb. The third empty place in the barley field was another symbol of Christ's great investment in us. Death was the penalty for sin. Our bodies would have lain in the grave until the Day of Judgment. After being resurrected to stand trial and receive sentence, we would have been cast into the lake of fire. Jesus took our place in the tomb.

While His body lay there, He descended into the lower parts of the earth (Ephesians 4:9) to defeat our spiritual enemies (Colossians 2:15) and to share the gospel with the Old Testament faithful (1 Peter 4:6). He swallowed up death with His abundant, inexhaustible life. Then He returned in time for His body to be resurrected on the same date the children of Israel had marched through the Red Sea to victory hundreds of years earlier.

He led a procession on this glorious Resurrection day. Many of the Old Testament saints were seen on the streets of Jerusalem (Matthew 27:52-54). Now they could go with Him into the presence of the Father. He demonstrated that His power was sufficient to resurrect the dead. That power is also sufficient to either resurrect or rapture us.

But He left an empty tomb. Don't ever forget the price Jesus paid: an empty throne, an empty cross, an empty tomb. We cost more than anything in the universe. We cost God His only begotten Son. We cost Jesus His throne, His life and a visit to hell. God was willing to pay for us to be His children. Jesus was willing to be our substitute. He was God's first-fruits gift to us.

Some people have been unwilling to tithe because it leaves an empty place . . . it costs them something. It is supposed to cost us! The empty place is a reminder of what it cost Jesus to take our place in judgment. Thank God for the empty place! May it ever remind us of the price Jesus paid. That is one of the reasons the firstfruits principle is forever. For all eternity we are to remember what He did. We will worship Him with extreme gratitude. We will celebrate His lordship forever. We will honor Him with our substance eternally.

Firstfruits and tithes have always been to Jesus. The Old Testament believer celebrated what Christ would do someday at Calvary. His lordship was demonstrated in the Feast of Firstfruits and in the bringing of the tithes. We New Testament believers have the privilege of honoring Him with our substance, looking back to the completed work of Christ. It was a terrible thing for the enlightened of Old Testament times to dishonor the Lord in refusing to sanctify all material possessions unto the Lord by tithing. How much greater is the rebellion now that Jesus' work is completed and revealed?

CHAPTER 7

ROBBING AND RECONCILING

God Has Given You the City

The children of the church all learn the exciting Bible story of Joshua's leading Israel into the Promised Land. Jericho was the first city they encountered upon crossing the Jordan. Because it was so well fortified, God performed a miracle to lower the walls. The miracle was predicated upon the obedience of the Israelites to walk around the city once a day for six days, and seven times on the seventh day.

Remember that on the sixth day of Creation man was created. That's why six is often considered the number which represents man. "Six days shalt thou labour," God commanded, "and on the seventh day thou shalt rest" (Exodus 20:9, 23:12). Six days men marched around the city of Jericho . . . and nothing happened. Even in our obedience we are still dependent upon God for results. The farmer may labor six days, working with the soil God created, the sunlight God has commanded, the rain God has sent, and the seed God has produced, but nothing will happen for all man's labor without the divine element.

On the seventh day they marched around the city seven times and then raised their voices in a shout of triumph because God had given them the city. At the time they shouted, God had only given them His word that He would give them the city. But because they had obeyed, and because God's word cannot be broken, it was appropriate, even expedient, for them to glorify God at this point. It is always appropriate to rejoice and praise God when we have obeyed His Word.

When they had given God their obedience, when they had done what they could do, although it had made no difference in the physical realm, it was making a tremendous difference in the world of the spirit. That's why the world doesn't obey God. They can't see into the world of the Spirit. Because they cannot see the spiritual difference, they have no faith that any material difference will occur.

The seventh day was God's day — reserved as a day of rest for man and a day of communion with God. So on the day dedicated to Him, and after faithfully marching in obedience to Him, God pulled the foundations out from under the great walls. They had to fall. The city was now exposed and vulnerable. Conquering the city was quite simple after God had moved. He had indeed given them the city. And this victory was an important key to conquering all of the other cities.

Firstfruits City

Although God gave them this strategic city, they gave it right back to Him, because this was a firstfruits city. "And the city shall be accursed [devoted], even it, and all that are therein, to the Lord. . . . And ye, in any wise keep yourselves from the accursed thing, lest ye make yourselves accursed, when ye take of the accursed thing, and make the camp of Israel a curse, and trouble it. But all the silver, and gold, and vessels of brass and iron, are consecrated unto the Lord: they shall come into the treasury of the Lord" (Joshua 6:17-19).

The firstfruits principle is so important that God required its observance immediately upon entering the Promised Land. The first city taken by conquest would be devoted to Him. It would be burned with everything in it as an offering to the Lord, except for gold, silver, iron, brass and the family of Rahab. The metals named would be placed in the treasury of the tabernacle. The city itself was not to be rebuilt.

The Hebrew word for *devoted* carries with it two opposite meanings. If that which is supposed to be devoted to the Lord is so presented to Him, then that act of consecration brings blessing upon the worshiper. But if that which God has claimed is not properly presented to Him, then it brings a curse.

The teaching's of Scripture are replete with examples:

- Adam and Eve ate from the forbidden tree and received the curse (3:22-24).
- Cain violated God's instructions regarding the devoted portion and smarted under God's rejection of him and his compromised offering (4:5-7).
- Abraham tithed correctly and was blessed greatly (14:20—15:1).
- Jacob received blessing the same way (28:20-22).
- Proverbs 3:9,10 restates the principle.
- Moses detailed the blessings and the curses in the Books of the Law.
- Nehemiah claimed the promise (13:31).
- Jeremiah used the principle as an illustration (2:3).
- Malachi identified their national problems with individual violations of this practice (3:9).
- Jesus commanded obedience to it (Matthew 22:21; 23:23).
- Paul described its blessing (Romans 11:16).
- The writer of Hebrews revealed the heavenly aspect of tithing as showing forth the preeminence of Christ (7:8).

Satan Hates Tithing

Satan is always quick to come against tithing. It is a

strategic necessity to him, and it is also a personal expediency to him. God let Abraham know after his greatest day of tithing and giving that he did not have to fear, because God would be his shield and his reward. Jacob prayed for God's provision and protection and in the same prayer pledged to be a faithful tither. We know that both of them realized the promise of blessing upon the tither.

Malachi preached that the curse was upon Israel because they were robbing God in consuming that which was devoted. He also promised that if they would repent and bring all the tithes and offerings unto God that God would rebuke the devourer for their sakes. That would remove the curse and bring the blessing of God to them.

Satan's greatest delight is to attack man, that which God has created in His own image. Our obedience to God in the handling of possessions entitles us to God's shield. When we disobey Him, we raise the prominence of created substance so that it gets in the way of our relationship with God. Although men look to wealth as a source of supply and protection, only God can really provide and protect in every circumstance. Thus, the elevating of mammon leaves us exposed to Satan's attack. He will always oppose tithing, then, because of the strategic necessity of having man's cooperation to remove this shield which keeps him out.

Remember that Satan's fall came as a result of his pride. He still has the "pride" problem. Now, imagine how embarrassing it must be for this megalomaniac to be personally rebuked by God Almighty. That is what God has promised will occur when you or I repent from our disobedience regarding tithes and offerings and walk in faithfulness.

Satan cannot resist the temptation to attack us anytime we have removed ourselves from God's protection. But he always runs the risk that we will get right with God, bring all the tithes and offerings to God's house, and then he will suffer the indignity and embarrassment of

God's public repudiation. Satan will always attack tithing—first, so that he can get at you through your disobedience if you act on his word instead of God's Word; secondly, for his personal expediency to avoid public humiliation and defeat.

An Idolater in God's Camp

Only one man responded to Satan's appeal on the day that Jericho was conquered. Achan decided to take some of the spoil and hide it in his tent. We don't know for sure what Achan was thinking. After all, God's word had been plain on the subject. He had witnessed the mighty power and the presence of God all of his life. He had just observed the power of God press the walls of Jericho into the ground. Surely he would not dare disobey this powerful God who had just judged Jericho for its sins and destroyed the whole city.

He may have decided that God really didn't need this stuff. That's a common justification today. He obviously thought he deserved it. And he may have even rationalized that he needed it for retirement. Or that he would use it to help the poor. Anyway, the tabernacle treasury didn't need it. And what good would it do to allow that expensive Babylonian garment to be burned up?

All kinds of excuses can be made. They are manufactured daily by those who do not want to release to God that which He has commanded. But none are acceptable.

Achan found it easier to put his trust in gold and silver than to continue to trust God. A real part of that temptation is based upon our hope that money will give us security but leave us in control. Whereas when we trust in God, we must yield to Him and be under His control. The temptation is appealing to our flesh, but it is cruelly deceptive.

Whatever I depend upon for my security is my god. If I am depending upon creation instead of the Creator, then I am an idolater. All idolatry is devil-inspired worship. Therefore it is of great consequence, as Achan would learn.

Achan's theft of the devoted materials occurred without a hitch. No one was aware that he had violated God's command—except his own family. He may have told them that one of the Jerichoans gave it to him, but they should keep it secret so the neighbors would not be jealous. How many devils do men release upon their families by the sins which they commit?

The Ai Surprise

After Jericho and that great victory, the next town westward was Ai. It was a little place and Joshua's reconnaissance reported that it would be easily defeated, not requiring more than 2,000 or 3,000 soldiers to take it.

Israel was shocked. Not only could they not defeat Ai, but the men of that little city put Israel's army to flight and killed 36 of their men. Joshua was stunned. He fell upon his face and pleaded with God.

Joshua asked why they had been brought into this land to be destroyed. He wished they had never crossed the Jordan. He realized that if God abandoned them they would never survive. Militarily their situation was extremely precarious. As word spread that Israel had been defeated by little Ai, the inhabitants of the land would be emboldened and inspired to come and destroy them. Joshua's desperation is revealed by his cry: "O Lord, what shall I say, when Israel turneth their backs before their enemies!" (Joshua 7:8).

Finally, to Joshua's prayer concerning their military plight, he added his concern for God himself. If the Canaanites destroy Israel and "cut off our name from the earth . . . what wilt thou do unto thy great name?" (v. 9).

As soon as Joshua got past his selfish interests and revealed his concern for the great name of God, God answered him. He told him to get up. He also told him what caused their problem.

Joshua's Old-fashioned Response to Trouble

I am fascinated with the difference in Joshua's reaction to problems and the reaction we give to church problems today. Joshua's first response was prayer. Our first response is usually to commission a new study of the problem. Joshua asked God what was wrong. We ask men. Joshua was ready to do what God said. We add another board or committee, start another training program, beef up the numbers and advertise more.

Joshua knew that better reconnaissance, increased training, more soldiers, and a survey or two wouldn't solve the problem. They needed God, and for some reason He wasn't with them.

If every believer would follow Joshua's example of earnest searching prayer, if every believer would genuinely repent, if we would get right with God financially, then revolutionary changes would occur. If all of God's tithe money were removed from retirement plans, bank accounts and investments and brought into God's house, there would be enough to do everything the church has been commanded to do. There have already been many spiritual casualties because of money stolen from God. But God in His mercy is allowing space to repent and reform. Next comes judgment.

God Answered the Inquiry

"Israel hath sinned, and they have also transgressed my covenant which I commanded them: for they have even taken of the accursed [devoted] thing, and have also stolen, and dissembled also, and they have put it even among their own stuff. Therefore the children of Israel could not stand before their enemies, but turned their backs before their enemies, because they were accursed: neither will I be with you any more, except ye destroy the accursed from among you" (v. 7:11, 12).

The military defeat at Ai could be explained in three words: *Israel hath sinned.* They transgressed God's commandment. They took for themselves spoils from the devoted (firstfruits) city. Because they took that which was devoted to God, they received a curse. Because of their sin, God's defense of them was removed. Although they did not understand the problem at the time of the battle, their confidence was gone. They couldn't fight for fear. They tried to run away.

Adam and Eve experienced the same phenomenon. When they sinned and took that which was devoted to God, they became fearful. They ran away to hide.

Proverbs 28:1 says, "The wicked flee when no man pursueth: but the righteous are bold as a lion."

God not only apprised Joshua of why His support had been withdrawn, He also declared that unless and until the matter was dealt with, He would not be with them anymore.

God's Answer for Our Defeat

This was written for our instruction. How many Christians have wondered why their lives are fearful, frustrated and powerless? Yet, whether from ignorance or willful disobedience, they have consumed the devoted portion entrusted to them, and the Spirit of God has withdrawn. Because of disobedience regarding the tithe, the Holy Spirit can only deal with them in conviction for their sin. But the Holy Spirit was sent not only to convince and convict of sin (John 16:8-11), He also came to fill you with power for the work of Christ in this world (Acts 1:8).

This is one of the most chronic causes of powerlessness in the lives of believers. It is vitally important that it be corrected now. If you feel your life in Christ is powerless and defeated and you can see how violating God's Word regarding the tithe has created this condition, if you would like to change it, then pray this prayer: "Father, I come in Jesus' name to thank You for the gospel of Christ and for Your call to me to become a part of Your family through the miracle of the new birth. I thank You also for convicting me of the sin of consuming the tithe instead of bringing it to You. Please forgive me this sin. I pledge to you that I will be faithful to your Word and that all you entrust to me will be promptly devoted to You through the tithe. I will show forth the lordship of Jesus in every part of my life. He will have the preeminence in everything. Now, Father, let Your Holy Spirit flow in me like a mighty river of life. Anoint my living and my praying. Make me victorious over my enemy because of Your power and presence in my life. I praise You for being my source and my shield. In Jesus' name. Amen."

The Corporate Dilemma

Achan's sin not only robbed him of the presence of God in his life, it also compromised the entire nation. We need each other. And we need each other to live right. The church is an army. When one soldier fails or falls, it encourages the Enemy. It gives the Enemy a door of opportunity to break through the lines and defeat us.

One of the problems prophesied for our time was "having a form of godliness, but denying the power thereof" (2 Timothy 3:5). Churches abound today, but for the most part they are powerless. When Christians practice, and churches condone, robbing God, they will always be powerless, just as Israel was at Ai.

You can help conquer this problem. As you faithfully live for God, encourage your pastor and other Christians to also practice the Word in their finances. Provoke them with love to study the Scriptures. Follow God's admonition to Joshua: "Be thou strong and very courageous . . . to do according to all the law" (Joshua 1:7). You will be helping to solve the power problem in the church and to prepare the church to again be victorious.

Another prophecy which applies to this present state of powerless churches is the one that warns us of seducing spirits and doctrines of devils (1 Timothy 4:1). You do not have to go to the cults, the occult or the New Agers to find doctrines of devils. God taught tithing and giving. Everyone who teaches against it is teaching doctrines of devils. Israel's experience at Ai and the church's experience in the 20th century provide us more than sufficient understanding of Satan's motive for coming against God's truth regarding tithing and giving.

Removing the Curse

"Up, sanctify the people, and say, Sanctify yourselves against to morrow: for thus saith the Lord God of Israel, There is an accursed thing in the midst of thee, O Israel: thou canst not stand before thine enemies, until ye take away the accursed thing from among you" (Joshua 7:13).

Knowing the problem is not sufficient. Talking about it doesn't fix it. God commanded that it must be dealt with promptly and properly.

How often have we acted as if having love and forgiveness means never to confront? The Bible gives guidance for all three and commands us to exercise them.

The children of Israel had to prepare themselves to deal with this sin. They had one day in which to sanctify themselves so they could cope with the discovering of the offender, the judgment of that individual and the execution. This man who had so brazenly disobeyed God would not be a monster. When he was identified to them, he would certainly be a son of Israel. He would be a member of one of their tribes. He would probably be a good neighbor to some of them. But his sin had already brought death to 36 men, and now everybody was in jeopardy until justice could be dispensed.

The people whose sins are pulling down our nation are often very popular. Some of them hold public office. Others wield great power as entertainers or through the mass media. Some are neighbors, some are pastors, some are church members. Sometimes it may be you or I.

Look how many "little battles" the church has lost in recent years. One woman withstood the church and had prayer removed from the schools. A few people persuaded the Supreme Court to legalize the murder of unborn babies. Homosexuals have defied the church's right to call their perversion sin, and they constantly promote legislation forbidding us to protect ourselves and our children from their recruitment efforts. Cities are forbidding churches to build where they wish, and some have outlawed religious meetings in homes.

God told Israel they could not stand before their enemies until they corrected their situation. We must set our financial houses in order so that we may again confront our enemies and triumph over them.

Judgment Day

Joshua followed the instruction of the Lord. In the morning all of the tribes presented themselves. God identified the tribe of Judah as the tribe of the offender. Then the families of that tribe presented themselves, and the family of Zerah was identified, then his son Zabdi, then Zabdi's son Carmi. Then the household of Achan was designated. This process God used was to teach them and us how sin implicates, embarrasses and hurts those most precious to us.

Joshua said to him, "Achan, My son, give, I pray thee, glory to the Lord God of Israel, and make confession unto him; and tell me now what thou hast done; hide it not from me" (v. 19). Joshua showed restraint and tenderness in this time of judgment. Surely he wanted Achan to repent before being executed.

Achan confessed that he had sinned against God. He told of the covetousness which had gripped him, how he took the devoted items and hid them in the ground inside his tent. Messengers were sent to his tent to retrieve the stolen treasure.

God had already given sentence for the offense. Achan, his sons, his daughters, his oxen, his donkeys, his sheep, his tent, the stolen goods and all that he had were stoned to death and then burned. After that the Lord turned from His anger.

Subsequently, Joshua and the children of Israel were victorious in their conquest of the cities of Canaan. A sad but powerful lesson was given to us. Robbing God is serious business. It is time for the church and every believer to honor the Lord with our substance. It is time to turn defeat and shame into victory and delight. It is time to conquer the land and claim the heathen for our inheritance.

CHAPTER 8

THE
TITHE

Under Law or Grace

Before we talk about the blessing available to the tither, we must consider the most common excuse Satan has offered for the refusal to tithe. Perhaps you have heard the authoritative-sounding disclaimer used by those opposed to tithing in an attempt to sweep away this teaching. They claim tithing was established under the law and therefore holds no validity for the New Testament church. This erroneous doctrine is used repeatedly to confuse the unlearned and in an attempt to "sanctify" the disobedient.

God in His great wisdom anticipated this error. He so beautifully refuted it with the Scriptures. Although tithing was practiced before Abraham, he was the one chosen by God to establish the foundational teaching in the Word. One of the reasons Abraham was used was to expose this "under the Law" error in our own day.

Abraham represents both Jews and Christians. He was the great patriarch through Isaac and Jacob of all Jews for all time. He is also the father of the faithful. He was a man of faith and is remembered in the "Hall of Faith" in the New Testament (Hebrews 11:8). Paul said, "And if ye be Christ's, then are ye Abraham's seed, and heirs according to the promise" (Galatians 3:29).

In Genesis 14 we have the man who represents the paying of tithes for both Old Testament believers and New Testament believers. He is a good example. And we are to honor our fathers . . . respect their example and instruction. Isn't it beautiful that the father of all the faithful is the one God used for His first teaching to us about tithing? This was His initial rebuttal to the present-day error. Abraham is father and example to the Jews and the Christians.

Jesus made use of this unique role of Abraham when He told the Jews who were so proud of their connection to Abraham: "If ye were Abraham's children, ye would do the works of Abraham" (John 8:39). Most Christians are delighted to know that we are also children of Abraham and heirs to the promise. Yet Jesus' challenge still holds: If you were Abraham's children, you would do the works of Abraham. We know that one of his works was tithing; another was giving.

In John 8:44 Jesus continued the dispute with the Jews and declared: "Ye are of your father the devil, and the lusts of your father ye will do. He was a murderer from the beginning, and abode not in the truth, because there is no truth in him. When he speaketh a lie, he speaketh of his own: for he is a liar, and the father of it." He continued: "He that is of God heareth God's words: ye therefore hear them not, because ye are not of God" (v. 47).

Obviously, Jesus spoke very plainly and forcefully. He left no room for misunderstanding concerning His meaning. He was dealing with life-and-death matters. And we must not misunderstand. We are dealing with the most serious issues of life, and there is no place for flippancy. The children of Abraham do the works of Abraham. He who is of God hears God's words.

Priest Forever

Melchizedek was the priest who received Abraham's tithes. Was he a priest established under the law of Moses? Absolutely not. The Levitical priesthood was in the loins of Abraham and was therefore subordinate to the priesthood of Melchizedek (Hebrews 7:9, 10). Was tithing then originated by the law of Moses? Of course not. The law of Moses could only embrace the tithe principle already established. The law and the Levitical priesthood always were subordinate to the priesthood of Melchizedek. Tithing preceded the law. The law had to embrace it. Tithing also succeeded the law, as we shall see in the New Testament.

Is the priesthood of Melchizedek still in effect under grace? What does the Bible say?

"Thou art a priest for ever after the order of Melchizedek" (Psalm 110:4; Hebrews 5:6; 6:20; 7:17, 21.)

"[Melchizedek] . . . made like unto the Son of God; abideth a priest continually" (Hebrews 7:3).

"For it is evident that our Lord sprang out of Juda; of which tribe Moses spake nothing concerning priesthood. And it is yet far more evident: for that after the similitude of Melchisedec there ariseth another priest, who is made, not after the law of a carnal commandment, but after the power of an endless life" (Hebrews 7:14-16).

"But this man, because he continueth ever, hath an unchangeable priesthood" (Hebrews 7:24).

Scripture gives adequate testimony that the priesthood of Melchizedek is endless. It also tells us who is the high priest of this endless priesthood—none other than our Lord Jesus himself (Hebrews 3:1; 5:10).

Now you see what a horrible error it is to misrepresent the tithe as under the control of the law and ended with the law. That error is intended to deny us the understanding of the marvelous priesthood of Jesus and prevent our worship of Him with the tithe. It is intended to take away the only scriptural means of bringing material possessions under the lordship of Jesus. The priesthood of Jesus after the order of Melchizedek is another scriptural refutation of the "end of the tithe" error.

Still another refutation of the error is provided by the calendar. Abraham's covenant of promise was more than four centuries before the law of Moses, as was the recorded example of his tithing. Paul observed in Galatians 3:17 that the law cannot cancel this covenant of promise with Abraham: "And this I say that the covenant, that was confirmed before of God in Christ, the law, which was four hundred and thirty years after, cannot disannul, that it should make the promise of none effect." The law of Moses did not originate tithing and does not have the power to end it. The law embraced this principle as it did many others it could not abrogate.

Tithing was taught to us through the example of Abraham, father of the Jews and the Christians. It is interesting that all believers today wish to claim the blessing of Abraham, but some object to following his example. Thus, they are deprived of one of the principles upon which his blessing abounded.

Tithing was to the endless priesthood of Jesus in the Old and New Testaments. The Levitical priesthood was subordinate to the priesthood of Christ in Abraham's example, thus establishing the right perspective of the practice under the law and afterward. Tithing is still to Jesus and will always be to Him. "And here men that die receive tithes; but there he receiveth them, of whom it is witnessed that he liveth" (Hebrews 7:8).

Tithing was taught to us four centuries before the law. Paul used that point to teach us that the law of Moses could not terminate the covenant of Abraham. And, of course, we know that it didn't. Those who rebel against the tithing principle must come against a great volume of scriptures and must cling to a false premise. Let's look at their premise now from logic.

The Law and Logic

The law of Moses declared, "Thou shalt have no other gods before me" (Exodus 20:3). Does God allow Christians to have other gods before Him? Certainly not. Wait a minute! We are under grace. The law does not pertain here. Why can't we have other gods?

Ridiculous, isn't it? But there's more.

"Thou shalt not kill" (v. 13). Does God allow Christians

to kill? After all, we are not under the law anymore.

"Thou shalt not steal" (v. 15). It's OK under grace, isn't it? Many Christians rob, God you know. It must be all right. "Thou shalt not bear false witness" (v. 16). That was serious sin back then. Now everybody does it. We're under grace, right?

"Thou shalt not covet" (v. 17). The New Testament calls it idolatry (Ephesians 5:5).

You get the point. Although we are not under the law, these same sins are still forbidden. The New Testament deals with them forthrightly. Jesus warned that unless our righteousness exceeds that of the Pharisees, we will all certainly not enter the kingdom of heaven. Apparently, then, we are still accountable for the spirit of the law. Grace gives us the strength to live in conformity to the righteousness of God and provides forgiveness in those times we fail, unless we try to use grace as a license to sin.

How can anyone reason that the God who purposed to conform us to Christ no longer has any standards for us? How can they reason that the practice of tithing is over because of grace? Where is that found in the Word of God? You can be sure it isn't there.

It is a false premise that the fulfilling of the law ended the tithe. But even if the premise were to be accepted for the purposes of discussion, it still cannot be substantiated by logic or Scripture.

Now we are ready to search the Scriptures for more concerning this ancient and endless principle that possessions are sanctified by bringing them under the lordship of Jesus Christ.

Superstitions

As America has declined spiritually, we have also witnessed the rise of another great superstition—gambling. For most of our history gambling was properly viewed as a great evil. Although there have always been those who indulged in this sin, it was properly viewed by society as evil and, therefore, a condemned activity. Most state and local governments have laws forbidding or curtailing its practice.

Now we have been set upon by a fresh wave of this plague. Politicians with consciences too calloused to be offended have joined with a godless media to promote and establish lotteries as an activity of the state. It is less than amusing to see the free publicity given to lotteries in each state that has succumbed. The hype about winners is designed to give us sufficient hope to give our money to the state. Don't ever expect them to tell any of the stories of those people who sacrificed and lost. Nor will they tell how many winners experience disastrous consequences within a short time as the economic distortion warps and destroys relationships.

The truth of the matter is, there are far better odds that we will die than that we will win a lottery. That's an extremely poor place to put money and an even worse place to put our hope. When we exercise such a foolish hope, we will gradually see our faith transferred to this cruel and evil god. He will not only require the unrewarded sacrifice of money but eventually our soul as well. Gambling is no small superstition. The involvement of the state in such an evil reveals how far from God our nation has moved and how closely we now resemble other heathen nations.

Every get-rich-quick scheme is a threat to our soul. It is the stock-in-trade of the confidence man. We will be safe from these con games when we place our hope in God and our faith in His Word. God doesn't want us suddenly rich. "He that hasteth to be rich hath an evil eye, and considereth not that poverty shall come upon him" (Proverbs 28:22).

Yes, God does want us to prosper. He wants us to grow in the power of His truth. He wants us to be increased in our capacity to know Him and to be more like Him. For that to happen, we must cooperate with Him and honor His purpose for our life. A superstitious practice of heathens that called for a kid being boiled in its mother's milk, along with magic rites, with the milk being used to sprinkle the fields and gardens was rebuked by Moses three times. "Thou shalt not seethe a kid in his mother's milk. Thou shalt truly tithe all the increase of thy seed, that the field bringeth forth year by year" (Deuteronomy 14:21, 22). He was protecting his people from the false hope of heathen practices and reminding them that there is a dependable way to be blessed. As we believe in God and obey His commandments, as we bring everything under the lordship of Christ, we will be blessed. No one has to be cheated or defeated. God is Creator. He is source. He is sustainer. It is in His power to bless us for faithfulness. It is His good pleasure to bless us. It is His promise. Let's allow Him to show His blessing in our life through our obedience. Let someone else show God's judgment for disobedience. Let it not be you or me.

Promptness

Moses taught his people to be prompt in bringing to God their firstfruits and tithes. This is a key ingredient to the rewards available to the tither. Until I have actually brought the tithe to God's house, I have not tithed. If I delay, I have not put God first. I will find procrastination to be deepening disobedience. It will not require much time for something else to place an urgent claim on the tithe money if I am found holding it. Then problems become the lord of my life instead of Christ. Some lives have illustrated that a reluctance to release the tithe to God's house will eventually become an inability to release it. By simply basing our security upon money instead of upon God, we will soon find that money has become our god. Putting God first by promptly bringing Him the tithe is a powerful defense against possessions taking lordship over us.

I have learned in my own life that tithing is easy if I give Him the first tenth but difficult if I put God somewhere down the line. Understanding from Scripture that God is to be first always, and it is my privilege to keep Him first in possessions through the tithe, I have established a habit. Every time I receive my paycheck, I deposit it in the bank. Then the first check I write will be the tithe. My family and I then take that check to the next worship service as part of our worship. It is a testimony of our desire to give Christ preeminence in everything. His blessings to my family and me have been abundant.

One pastor had a businessman in his congregation who had been prospered greatly. Because the man's income was so large, he had begun having difficulty over his tithes. Finally, he came to the pastor and explained that although he had promised God to tithe at the time of his conversion, he was having difficulty continuing because the amount was now so large. He wanted to know if there was any way out of this dilemma.

The pastor assured him that he understood and, yes, there is a way out—through prayer. The businessman was so pleased that his pastor understood and that he could be freed from his responsibility. He got down on his knees ready for the prayer.

"Dear Lord," said the pastor, "I want you to reduce this man's income back to the level where tithing will be comfortable for him again."

The businessman began tapping the pastor on the shoulder to interrupt the prayer. When the pastor responded to him, he hurriedly commented, "I can pay my tithes at this level of income pastor. You don't need to pray anymore."

Although this is a humorous anecdote, it illustrates quite vividly the ease with which some people forget the fundamentals of this relationship with the Lord and His church. Wouldn't you be glad to pay a million dollars in tithes? That would be a sure indication that God had entrusted you with $10 million.

CHAPTER 9

COMMON QUESTIONS

Three Tithes

Another point of confusion concerning tithing was the practice under Moses' instructions of paying three tithes. The first was the tithe that sanctified the possessions and brought them under the lordship of Christ (Leviticus 27:26-32). The second was to pay the tither's expenses for his three visits to Jerusalem each year (Deuteronomy 14:23-26). He was expected to be there for the Feasts of Passover, Pentecost and Trumpets. Of course, there was a good deal of expense involved with travel even in those days. God instructed them to set this portion aside for the expenses of these feast times and to enjoy good food and drink as well.

The third tithe was only set aside every three years. It was calculated on the third year's income after the first two tithes had been computed. The Jew was expected to contribute that third-year tithe to the poor and needy with special consideration for widows and orphans (Deuteronomy 26:12-15). This involved him in helping the helpless. It was an ongoing demonstration of the principle: "blessed to be a blessing." This third tithe every three years would average close to 3 percent per year. After giving God the first tithe (10 percent) and allocating a second tithe for travel expenses to the feasts, the Jew gave to the poor an amount nearly equal to the total giving of many Christians today.

These second and third tithes never were considered as sacred and important as the first tithe for obvious reasons. However, the effect they had was quite worthy indeed. The faithful steward would not only sanctify all in his trust, but he would not be tempted to miserliness because the second tithe was to be spent on himself. He would have ample opportunity to remain charitable to the poor because he was to give about 3 percent of his income per year to those in need.

We would do well to set aside an adequate amount to attend Christian conferences, seminars and special meetings. That money is not wasted which we invest in worship, learning and fellowship.

Just as the first tithe is not the end of our giving but simply the proper beginning, 3 percent is not adequate for most of us to give to help the poor. But it would certainly be a good beginning. The law was a schoolmaster to help us establish good perspective and understanding. Grace will enable us not only to fulfill what we have learned from this great school but to exceed it.

Grace and Works

The church seems to have struggled with grace and works for most of its existence. One group will be so sold out to grace that they believe any mention of works is heresy. Another will be so works dependent that they suffer great condemnation if they are not producing enough of the right kinds of activity at all times. Stewardship understanding and practice are greatly affected by either extreme.

Paul sought to bring us to a balanced awareness of how grace and works are to coexist. Ephesians 2:8, 9 are frequently quoted to emphasize grace: "For by grace are ye saved through faith; and that not of yourselves: it is the gift of God: not of works, lest any man should boast." That is a wonderful scripture, and its message is cause for rejoicing.

Now read verse 10: "For we are his workmanship, created in Christ Jesus unto good works, which God hath before ordained that we should walk in them." That message is just as wonderful as the one before. Actually, they are two parts to the same message. The second part is usually neglected by anyone who is overstressing grace. Let's look at the beautiful balance Paul is offering.

Of course, we could not pay the debt of sin. Only God could save us by pouring out His wrath upon Christ to satisfy the demands of His justice. We couldn't construct a solution to our dilemma. We could not change our sin nature. Only God could do that by His amazing grace revealed in the offering of Jesus. We couldn't find God. He found us and gave us the good news of salvation simply through faith in Jesus. Then He even gave us the faith so we could believe. Salvation is not by man's work; it is the grace of God.

By His grace I have been redeemed that I might do good works. To stop at the redemption by grace is to retard the beautiful calling of Jesus for us to follow Him, to be His body upon the earth, to stand in Christ's stead. We are not working for our salvation; we are working because of it. The good works are the fruit borne out of the relationship. His works through us testify of His life in us.

Adam was not working for salvation either. He had a good relationship with God. He had no sin problem. The Tree of Life was always within his reach. Until he violated the trust God had given him, his life was perfect. God's grace was abundantly manifested in their relationship. His good works were the proper fruit of their relationship.

Wrongful Submission

Adam's disobedience upset the relationship. When he acted upon the fraudulent word of a created being in conflict with the word of the Creator, he subordinated himself to a created being greatly inferior to God. He abandoned the truth. Immediately it was reflected in his stewardship. The fruit produced of this new alliance was rebellion, fear, selfishness—the very nature of Satan began to be manifested in man. Of course, his works revealed what was happening in his spirit. It was necessary for God to judge man for his own benefit and to give him the motive and opportunity to repent.

Our relationship with God is a testimony to His grace. Each of us has given Him adequate justification to judge us and turn us over to the destroyer. But He doesn't. He continues to work patiently with us. He has given us each a stewardship assignment. We are stewards of His grace and His material resources too.

It is not uncommon to hear some Christians claim they are under grace. Therefore, God owns it all. Under the law they thought God only owned 10 percent. We go way beyond that, they say; we know He owns it all.

Believe it or not, people who talk like that are often trying to excuse themselves from tithing. However, the Old Testament believer well knew that God owns it all. The first verse in the Bible tells how He obtained it. Adam saw God demonstrate ownership rights. Abraham declared God is possessor of heaven and earth. He was echoing Melchizedek's proclamation of God's ownership found in Genesis 14. God continues His claim of ownership throughout Scripture. No, the Old Testament believer was not confused about God's ownership.

Words or Works

James observed that some are inclined to limit their good deeds to words. If a brother comes to us in need and we say to him, "Be warmed and fed," but we give him no assistance, what good is it? "Even so faith, if it hath not works, is dead, being alone" (2:17).

The same is true with God. If we have received God's grace, we will have faith. When we have a vital faith, it will produce the fruit of good works, not just words. We will not give lip service to God's ownership and grace. We will demonstrate His ownership through the tithe. We will prove that grace, not greed, is the motivating force in our lives.

I have had the privilege of working with hundreds of pastors. I have yet to hear one of them disagree on this point: Christians who tithe are also the most generous givers. There

84

are always a few who want to talk about grace, about God's total ownership, about giving much more than the tithe. But most of them just talk. The tithers consistently outgive them. As James said, "Show me your faith without your works, and I will show you my faith by my works" (James 2:18, *NKJV*).

Our stewardship shows what is really going on inside, in our spirits. No matter how well we talk, our works will either confirm or deny our faith. That's why Jesus said, "Let your light so shine before men, that they may see your good works, and glorify your Father which is in heaven" (Matthew 5:16).

We are not to make a show of our stewardship, but our works are to match our faith. Good works are the fruit of our relationship. The world loves fruit. God has chosen us to bear it for their blessing, His glory and our fulfillment. Abraham did not make a show of his tithing. Neither did he hide it. His example has proved to be priceless for us. Our own stewardship proves the Word of God is true and provides an irrefutable example for all who know us.

Legalism

Another charge sometimes leveled against tithers by nontithers is that we are being *legalistic*. Perhaps we should require that they define what they mean by the term before we try to answer the charge. Of course, there is a mean condition which answers to this title and none of us want the affliction nor the responsibility to defend it. There is also the tendency to apply negative labels to anything we would rather not do so that we may excuse ourselves from the responsibility with as little guilt as possible.

I honestly thought my dad was legalistic in his requirements that I eat all the food on my plate, do so with good manners, and never complain about the provisions or their preparation. I was sure Mom had the same problem. She required baths at scheduled times. Ears, necks and fingernails were regularly inspected. Judgments were made. Punishments were both corrective and memorable. I profited by their standards and enforcement.

Several of my uncles were farmers. They seemed to have this problem with legalism too. They were adamant about when to plow and how carefully it was done. They were dogmatic about what was planted in their fields. They were intolerant of weeds, worms and laziness. If you agreed to help, you did it their way.

Mom and Dad convinced me, over the years, that training children is serious business. I learned I had personal value through a childhood of intensive involvement by my parents in what I did and how I did it. Waiting until I was grown to make my own decisions about cleanliness, responsibility and church attendance never occurred to them. Now I can see that without their strict training with love I would be unable, as an adult, to make those decisions. I would not have the strength, experience or other fundamentals that must be developed during those formative years.

Those uncles who were so determined to farm correctly may have appeared legalistic to us kids, but if they had missed the season, they would have been destroyed economically. A lackadaisical attitude toward the harsh realities would have been very unwise. Now I am thankful for their diligence and discipline. It is especially meaningful to me when I see today's chaos in business, education, government and church, largely produced by people who have thrown out the underlying principles.

God has given principles in His Word which are as reliable now as they were 50 years or 500 years ago. They work for the parent, the farmer, the educator, the businessman, the politician, the church or for us.

Every discipline was built upon principles. The pilot who takes a casual attitude toward the principles of aeronautics will not take many hours of flying before he destroys himself. Politicians who disregard the principles of government will soon have unbalanced budgets, inflation, ever-increasing taxes and uncensored lawlessness. Judges who disrespect the law encourage violence and crime. Educators who deny the truth produce students with low self-esteem and poor performance in academics as well as in the marketplace. Parents who rear children absent the influence of love and discipline produce confused and frustrated adults. All around us are the pitiful examples of what happens when we abhor principles and the discipline necessary to build upon them (see Hosea 4:6).

No, following the scriptures on tithing does not constitute legalism. Adhering to God's principles constitutes righteous living. Legalism is creating laws apart from or beyond the laws of God and then trying to coerce obedience to them. If we allow the world to deprive us of building on the sure foundation of God's principles just by calling us legalists, then we have no chance of fulfilling our potential.

Rock or Sand

Jesus said we should build upon the rock and not upon the sand. What a profound illustration He gave us! Jesus is called the Rock. He is also the Truth. He is the Word. He does not change. He does not move. As we build our lives upon Him, we can withstand the storms that are sure to come. To build anywhere other than on Him is to build on sand. Then when trouble comes, we will fall.

The principle of tithing is revealed in His Word. As we have seen earlier, tithing has always been to Jesus for the purpose of bringing material possessions under His lordship. Of course, the law of Moses embraced tithing. It would have ignored or denied truth if it had not. We are faced with the same choice: deny truth or embrace it; build upon the Rock or upon the sand.

Nehemiah came to Jerusalem at a time when the disobedience of God's Word had left the nation in ruins. America is presently in decline for the same reason and, without a great revival, has no good end in sight. Nehemiah not only rebuilt the city, he restored tithing, established the right relationship of things and rebuilt their relationship with God (Nehemiah 10:35-39). As he closed his book, he asked God to remember him for his offerings and firstfruits (Nehemiah 13:31). He had reestablished the principles of truth in Jerusalem and brought the lordship of Christ into preeminence through firstfruits and tithes.

Discipline

Discipline has come under ruthless attack in our century. Many times the attackers are from among those who should know better. Beginning with the opposition to discipline in child rearing and continuing with opposition to discipline in education, we could not but produce multitudes unable to manage their own lives. Industry has become so appalled at the illiterate graduates entering the work force that they must try to educate them and work them at the same time. Small wonder we find ourselves at extreme disadvantage in the highly competitive international marketplace. Any nation that has held on to the discipline principle finds it can easily outperform us.

Discipline is the key to real freedom. The disciplined pilot has the freedom to fly safely and reap the rewards of travel at high speeds. The disciplined businessman has the freedom which comes from profits accrued from meeting a need in society. The disciplined farmer harvests the results of his faithful labor. The disciplined teacher has the fulfillment of seeing young lives made productive. The disciplined parent has the freedom to give to God and to society well-balanced and strong children. The disciplined steward is the one who is free to manage a portion of God's property without selfishness, covetousness or disobedience. And he is free to answer to God without fear or shame.

Those who attack discipline do so by pointing to the misuse of discipline. They then proceed to throw out the principle of discipline because of those incidents of abuse. That is really nonsense. We should give no more audience to such nonsense than we would if they demanded that we stop drinking water because so many have drowned in water.

The continuing distortion of valid principles will accelerate as the spirit of antichrist achieves increasing dominance in this society. He is the spirit of lawlessness. Christ who created all things gave us law (principles) just as He established law for the universe to follow. Antichrist is opposed to law because it is a revelation of the goodness and wisdom of Christ. The opposition to Christ and His law is a temporary situation. We must not be a party to such opposition.

This spirit of lawlessness has also reached into the church. Nowhere is it more apparent and more easily measured than in the area of stewardship. Christ's law concerning the receiving, managing, giving and spending of material resources has seen many attacks. They are of the same kind of nonsense the Enemy has used to persuade society into lawlessness. But the Christian should not be so easily deceived. We believers are to be unconditionally committed to God's Word, not the word of the world. We are to listen to the Holy Spirit, not the unholy spirit. We are to be masters of the material, not slaves to it. We are to prove the truth of God's way, not be objects of His judgment. We are blessed to be a blessing.

CHAPTER 10

THE TITHE BLESSING

The Covenant

The last book of the Old Testament contains a powerful presentation on tithing. It is most often referred to because of its great promise of blessing. We certainly want to understand that portion. However, several lessons surround the promise of blessing. We can profit by all of them.

Malachi the prophet began by telling Israel that he had the burden of the word of the Lord to them (Malachi 1:1). How can something as wonderful as God's Word be a burden? Because it discerns the thoughts and intentions of our hearts (Hebrews 4:12). It shines the light of truth on all the darkness of evil that has come into our lives (Psalm 119). It calls for us to change (repent) so that God may bless us and make us a blessing to others.

Every prophet called the people back to the covenant relationship with God. Moses explained the reason God gave us the power to get wealth. "But thou shalt remember the Lord thy God: for it is he that giveth the power to get wealth, *that he may establish his covenant* which he sware unto thy fathers, as it is this day" (Deuteronomy 8:18). God establishes His Word in us as we receive it and *act* upon it. He establishes His Word in the world by demonstrating it to the world through our lives. The world is generally more interested in money than any other subject. As they see the example of our life and how we follow a specific financial plan, that we are blessed, our needs met, yet we are unselfish, they are seeing God's Word in action. It costs money to operate the church and its ministries. Its mission is to establish the covenant; that is, preach and live the Word. God gave you and me the power to get wealth to fund that great mission.

Twins in Opposition

Malachi's message moved immediately to a great biblical example of two brothers: Jacob and Esau. Both were sinners. The Bible makes that point indisputably. But Jacob had a heart for God; Esau did not. Jacob placed high value on the blessing and presence of God; Esau disdained it. Jacob's life suffered from his penchant for deception. He reaped a very painful harvest for it, but he was repentant. Esau sought repentance, but he had rebelled for so long and his heart had become so hard he just couldn't change.

Jacob desired the blessings of God in his life. Look at his prayer in Genesis 28:20-22: "And Jacob vowed a vow, saying, If God will be with me, and will keep me in this way that I go, and will give me bread to eat, and raiment to put on, so that I come again to my father's house in peace; then shall the Lord be my God: and this stone, which I have set for a pillar, shall be God's house: and of all that thou shalt give me I will surely give the tenth unto thee."

He recognized God as his source of supply and the giver of all blessings. He desired God's presence in his life. He honored the house of God, and he vowed to be a tither. We know God answered his prayer. Although he suffered consequences for his sins, he received the protection and provision made available through God's Word. He was a blessed tither.

The contrast of the lives of these two brothers is a powerful lesson to us all. It is proof of God's Word. Each of us will follow a similar pattern of one or the other of these brothers. If you have a heart for God, like Jacob, you are blessed.

Dishonoring God

Next, Malachi dealt with the problem of backslidden religious leaders. "A son honoureth his father, and a servant his master: if then I be a father, where is mine honour? And if I be a master, where is my fear? saith the Lord of hosts unto you, O priests, that despise my name. And ye say, Wherein have we despised thy name?" (Malachi 1:6).

God proceeded to answer His own question. He detailed how they have been contemptible toward Him in their offerings. He declared that He had no pleasure in them and that He would not receive an offering from them. Then He began to talk about us Christians in verse 11: "My name shall be great among the Gentiles; and in every place incense shall be offered unto my name, and a pure offering: for my name shall be great among the heathen, saith the Lord of hosts."

Isn't that interesting? God's disappointment with the Jews and their disrespect of His name as evidenced by their offerings provoked Him to look forward to our time. He anticipated that we would honor Him, make His name great and give Him pure offerings.

Jesus taught us to call God our Father (Matthew 6:9). We receive great comfort from that Father/child relationship, and well we should. But how do we respond to God's question, "If then I be a father, where is mine honour?" Remember the command in Proverbs 3:9: "Honour the Lord with thy substance, and with the firstfruits of all thine increase." He expects us to do better than the Jews. He commands us to honor Him with all the substance He entrusts to us. He expects us to put Him first as demonstrated in the practice of tithing. Disobedience is dishonoring. Obedience is honoring.

Cursing

God then talked about a curse upon the deceitful giver and a curse He would send upon the blessings. In chapter 3 He declared that the whole nation was cursed for robbing Him in tithes and offerings. There was much evidence of the curse. Israel was coming undone as a nation. Beginning with profane priests, a plague of divorce, crooked businessmen, deceitful worshipers and brazen blasphemers, the fabric of society was unraveling. Israel had many similarities to our own time. We can now clearly see that America's blessings are becoming cursed.

But God is long-suffering and merciful. His judgment was to give them an opportunity to see the product of their sinful ways and motivate them to return to Him. They had begun to ask the question, "Wherein shall we return?" (Malachi 3:7).

They had need for many changes, but they needed a starting place for spiritual reform. God gave it to them. "Bring ye all the tithes into the storehouse, that there may be meat in mine house, and prove me now herewith, saith the Lord of hosts, if I will not open you the windows of heaven, and pour you out a blessing, that there shall not be room enough to receive it" (Malachi 3:10). Financial reform is a good first step in spiritual reform for the backslider.

Solomon said, "But money answereth all things" (Ecclesiastes 10:19). Since money is the universal medium of exchange, it represents all things material. When we subordinate money to the lordship of Christ, it is as if we have put all the material things in our control under His authority. Through the tithe we have brought truth to bear upon the spiritual challenge of proper order in our relationship to things.

God said to bring the tithes into the storehouse because this is the method He has chosen to fund the operation of His house. God's preferred method of honoring Him with the tithe is to bring it with us as we come to church to worship Him.

One puffed-up fellow said he would bring the tithe when the church built a storehouse to receive it. I responded that when his income was all in livestock and produce, then the church would accommodate him, but as long as his income was money, his tithe should be in money. The church really doesn't need a barn to house cash and checks.

God said bring *all* the tithes to His house. Tithe means a tenth. Until we have accurately counted the tenth of all our increase and brought it to Him, we still haven't tithed.

Gross or Net

Some people tithe on their gross income, and others tithe on the net. Some teachers declare that it must be gross, others say net. I suspect this is one of those areas where each individual should ask the Lord for direction. But I will venture an opinion.

When the Word said tithe the increase, I believe that in most cases that would mean net. A Filipino businessman asked me this question. When I responded that many Christians tithe from the gross, his face showed great consternation. He was a new Christian and eager to follow the Lord in everything, but he thought he had just encountered his undoing. In his experience he had rarely netted more than 10 percent in the operation of his business. He would not have enough money to pay tithes on the gross. His great alarm was that tithing would cost him his faith. When I assured him the Scripture calls for the tithe on the increase, he was relieved and very pleased to follow the Word in tithing.

We have also had in times past, in the United States, income tax rates in excess of 90 percent for the larger incomes. In nations that do not allow a charitable deduction, such a tax circumstance could prevent an individual from paying tithes on the gross amount of his income.

Sharecroppers traditionally divide the produce of the farm with the landowner. To require him to tithe the gross amount would be to compute his tithe as 20 percent of that entrusted to him. The tax structure has tended to make sharecroppers of us all in that the government takes such a substantial portion through prior claims.

Partners in business are called by the Scriptures to tithe. But each partner would not tithe on the gross. Each is responsible to tithe and give from his share. In a similar way, the government enters into partnership with us. We are each responsible to tithe and give from our share—not for the government and its portion. We must keep integrity with God. That means to obey the Word without overdoing or underdoing.

Jesus appeared to be allowing for this when He said, "Render . . . unto Caesar the things which are Caesar's; and unto God the things that are God's" (Matthew 22:21).

Jesus was not compromising the tithe principle of putting God first in our lives. But He was recognizing that the government position with the tax is like the landowner's position with his share of the produce. The government's portion is never mine to begin with. I am charged to pay the legally assessed tax, but I have no say over that money—it's never really mine. I am taught to pay tithes on all that is entrusted to me and to my discretion.

However, God does not limit Himself to the tithe and freewill offerings. Because He is the owner He may ask for any amount, or all of it, at anytime. Many Christians have experienced that call from God: the church at Jerusalem, Stanley Tam and thousands of others. Their lives show that anyone who receives an extraordinary call from God is in for extraordinary blessing through obedience to that call to do more than the ordinary.

Robbery

Governments take a very dim view of tax *evasion*. Tax *avoidance* should be practiced by everyone through every legal means, but there is no legal way to *evade* taxes. One lawyer was asked to explain the difference between tax avoidance and tax evasion. He answered, "About 15 years."

God takes a very dim view of tithe evasion. He calls it *robbery*. He goes so far as to say it is robbing God (Malachi 3:8). It is hard to imagine any reasonably intelligent criminal setting out to rob someone far more powerful than himself, especially if his chance of getting away is absolutely zero. God has all power. He has all knowledge. No one can get away from Him. Yet many attempt to rob Him every week, and some of them claim to be His children.

Robbery is violation of a moral law. Nowhere does the New Testament authorize God's children to live in conflict with any portion of the moral law of the Old Testament. To rob someone is to demean that person, to show disrespect and dishonor. God inquires of all those who despise Him, "Where is mine honour?" (Malachi 1:6). Do you believe any person would ask God for His protection on the highway while riding in a car purchased with money stolen from God? Do you believe anyone would have the audacity to ask God for His care and protection while they sleep in a house paid for with money illegally taken from the one to whom they pray? It happens every day.

I sometimes encourage people to select a different victim if you have an overpowering urge to rob someone. Even a few bank robbers get away, temporarily. But there is no way any person can get away with robbing God. Surely there are no Bible teachers who will teach that you can be a Christian robber. Even the ones who are confused about tithing will not approve robbery. God said that's exactly what it is when we do not bring Him all the tithe.

Who Is Your Source?

Several years ago a young pastor invited a guest speaker to his church. As the pastor visited with his guest, he shared what a tough time they were experiencing financially. The older minister asked the young pastor about his belief and practice of tithing. The pastor said he felt that it was a good thing to do, but he rarely ever did it personally.

His guest responded, "Let me give you the advantage of my own experience. If you will give God the first tenth of all that comes to you, I will back you financially. Any month in which you do not have enough for your necessities, all you need to do is call me. I will promptly send you the money to meet your need." The pastor agreed to do it.

Months later when they had their next opportunity to visit, the older minister inquired about his financial circumstances.

"We are doing fine," said the young pastor. "But," he continued, "there's more to the story. Your offer gave me the confidence to become a tither. However, one day while I was praying, God asked me a most challenging question: 'How can a man's guarantee supported by very limited resources give you the confidence to obey My Word when you did not have the confidence to obey knowing that My Word is backed by My unlimited resources?' "

The young pastor repented in response to God's convicting question. He now tithes with the joyful confidence that God is his source and all he must do is obey God. We may all be blessed with that marvelous truth. God told backslidden Israel to repent, not just in words but in deeds. Bring all the tithes to God, put Him first, and He will be your source. "Prove me now herewith."

Proving God

Throughout the Bible, God places the principle of faith foremost in receiving from Him. Here is an interesting exception. God challenges us: Prove Me now. It is as if He is so intent on our learning this great truth that He dares us to try it.

God wants us to enjoy having our needs met. He wants us to know He is able and willing to provide for us. He wants us to be free from bondage to material things. He wants us to know the freedom of having everything under the lordship of Jesus. So He says to prove Him: Tithe!

What does He say will happen when we prove Him through our obedience? He will open the windows of heaven. Heaven is a place of plenty and a place of beauty. Gold is used for asphalt in heaven—and not the cheap gold we are used to seeing. God uses a gold so pure it is translucent, and He uses it to pave streets.

Is God going to tear up the streets to enrich us when we tithe? Goodness no! He has riches aplenty besides the building materials. He has promised to meet all our needs according to His riches in glory by Christ Jesus.

Don't make the mistake of looking at earthly limitations.

God has committed the riches of heaven to us now. Apparently, God has a bank that cannot exhaust its riches. He doesn't need them. They are for His obedient children.

One morning I walked into a bank. The front door was open to let us in from the cold, but the teller windows weren't open yet. As we waited for the windows to open so we could do business, the thought suddenly struck me. The windows of God's bank are open to serve the tither . . . at all times.

Would you expect a local bank to pay you interest on money you never deposited at that bank? Of course not. Yet some expect God to bless them although they never make any deposits at God's house.

God describes the blessing available to the tither as abundant. He said it would be so big we would not have room to receive it. Most of us feel we need that blessing, and we are tempted to cry out, "Try me!" But God says we are supposed to try Him.

God is a God of abundance, but He is not a God of wastefulness. I have watched in my own life how God has blessed me according to my capacity. As I grow in my capacity to be trusted, He entrusts more to me. The tither is receiving his needs met and he is receiving the good things of God according to his capacity. The windows of heaven are always open to the tither.

Tithing and Fishing

Junior Hardin lives in Fort Pierce, Florida. He makes his living with a 51-foot fishing boat. He called his wife one day to tell her he was about to depart on a fishing run and wanted to know if they had their tithes paid up to date.

His wife admitted she was holding the tithe money in the checking account because that $280 was all they had. He said, "Take it to the church. You know I can't go fishing owing tithe money to the Lord."

When he and his crew found fish, they were in rocky shoals where the boat could not safely go. As they maneuvered near, they struck a rock which pierced a large hole in the hull. The boat began taking on quantities of seawater and listed heavily to one side. The men were struggling to hold on when Junior cried out, "Lord, I'm a tither. You said you would rebuke the devourer for a tither." Immediately the boat was lifted off the rock and began to right itself. They quickly shoved the bilge pump in the hole and began pumping water out of the boat. Just as things began to look promising, the pump motor stopped. They had run out of gasoline. The boat engines ran on diesel. There was no more gasoline on board.

As the water poured in around the pump motor stuck in the hole in the boat, Junior prayed again . . . very loudly. "Dear Lord, You got us off the rock and righted the boat, but unless You help us, we will still sink. This old boat is the only way I have to make a living. Somehow, Lord, save us and save this old boat."

The water stopped coming in. They made it back to dock. Later, when the boat was repaired, they returned to where they had sighted the fish. They were still confining themselves to the shoals. He let down his nets anyway, although that's not the way to catch fish. With passive nets the fish would have to catch themselves. And they did.

When they began to haul in the nets, they had more fish than they could store in their boat. They called to another boat for help. They shared the surplus fish with them and then headed for home. Upon selling their catch, they received $28,000. Junior's last tithe check had been $280. What a coincidence! Or, rather, what a demonstration of God's Word!

The Devourer

Jesus informed us that the thief (Satan) comes only to steal, to kill and to destroy (John 10:10). When we are disobedient to God, we give our enemy the opportunity to come against us. When we rob God, we place ourselves under the influence of "the thief." We are subjecting ourselves to him by our own actions. The problem is one of major dimensions. God created us with such a high purpose and calling. We are to enjoy His gift of Himself to us in a wonderful relationship.

We experience truth through our worship of Him. We realize growth through our obedient service to Him. We should hate anything that subverts or distorts this marvelous relationship.

Satan has learned that fallen man has an insecurity. When the relationship with God was interrupted, man began to seek for security in things. The enemy of our souls constantly agitates the insecurity and proffers materialism as the answer to our need. If we take the bait, Satan wins. We begin to move into slavery.

When man's heart is sold out for possessions, he eventually becomes possessed. He is no longer the faithful steward honoring God through his obedience and glorifying God through his freedom. He is a slave. God's high purpose for that individual has become inverted. Instead of ruling over God's creation as a child of God, he himself is ruled by that which was created lower than himself.

Unwittingly, this man has become a worshiper of Satan the deceiver instead of God the divine. Unless he is rescued from this prison by the gospel, his end is sure and tragic. Just because his handcuffs are forged with gold makes him no less a prisoner than the individual bound with a baser substance. Even though the world admires and compliments his fine taste in expensive shackles, Satan holds him prisoner . . . a prisoner who rarely understands why he is in so much grief.

Some years ago a missionary returned to America after laboring for an extended time in a Third World nation. He was surprised to see the evidence of so much financial prosperity, especially in the church. As he traveled from church to church to give his report, he dared not be critical. But in a letter to his wife, who was still on the field attending to their work, he wrote: "Everyone has treated me very kindly. The thing that gets to me the most is that I see so many Bible schools and churches worn around the necks and upon the fingers of our Christian brothers and sisters."

I remember the shock I experienced to see a well-dressed man handcuffed to a plainclothes policeman in an airport. But I have since observed well-dressed Christians handcuffed to their possessions. It is a sad dilemma. People who have experienced the spiritual freedom paid for by Jesus Christ can become entrapped by materialism. The purpose of their stewardship becomes obscured. They live as if they are blessed to bless themselves, and the handcuffs are locked tightly on their wrists.

That is not to condemn those to whom God has entrusted abundance because of their faithful obedience to Him. Some exemplary Christians are wealthy. But they remember they are stewards, not owners. And they are quick to obey the Lord in any distribution of that which He has entrusted to them. God has some stewards with great faith, great ability and great resources. They do not waste those resources upon themselves but faithfully use them for the glory of God.

God promised to "rebuke the devourer" for the sake of a tither. Actually, the act of tithing itself is a rebuke to Satan. This act declares the lordship of Jesus over the worshiper, it declares the stewardship of the believer over that which has been entrusted to him, and it subordinates the possession under God's Word and under God's servant.

No wonder Satan resents the tithe. It cuts him off from his most productive avenue to deceive and enslave us . . . the avenue of materialism. He is also aware that God's promise to rebuke him is no idle threat. He has been rebuked constantly by God on behalf of the tither for thousands of years.

God Raises Cotton

Arlie Rogers lives in Selma, California. His friends refer to him as the "sweet potato king" out of respect for his great farming operation. Arlie is one of the best examples of faithfulness over great resources that I have ever seen. But today's prosperity is the result of faithfulness over small things in the past.

When Arlie and his brother first moved to California, they worked long and hard to accumulate enough to buy one piece of the rich San Joaquin farmland. After years of working and waiting, they finally obtained a farm. The money crop was cotton, so they invested everything they had sowing cotton. When the young cotton plants were out of the ground good, a sandstorm blew through the valley and killed everybody's cotton.

Arlie called his pastor to come out to the farm. They walked with Pastor Burnham out to look at the disaster. They explained to him, "Everything we had was in that crop. We don't have any money or credit left to replant. We are completely ruined. Now we will lose everything."

Pastor Burnham responded, "No, fellows, it's really not that bad. The God we serve raised His own Son from the dead after three days. I know He can raise cotton."

With that statement the pastor got down on his knees in the dirt of the cotton field and prayed a simple little prayer. "Father, these men are tithers. You said You would rebuke the devourer for a tither. I am asking You to manifest the power of Your Word and fulfill that promise right here in this cotton field. Bring this cotton back and give these men a good crop. In Jesus' name. Amen."

"That ought to take care of it," he said. Then he brushed the dirt off of his pants and headed back to town.

A few days later the Rogers brothers called him back to see a miracle. God did rebuke the devourer. They did have a good crop. They had a pastor who knew how to pray a prayer of faith. They served a God who is faithful to His Word. And they were believers who were also faithful to the Word. They were tithers. Satan was defeated.

Arlie has been blessed to be a blessing . . . and he is.

Satan is still the devourer. He is the thief who comes to steal, kill and destroy. He sponsors inflation through undisciplined and unprincipled politicians. The value of money is being devoured. Satan hopes inflation will produce such fear in the hearts of believers that they will stop supporting the work of the church. Yet our greatest defense against inflation is to tithe. Then we have the right to claim God's promise that He will rebuke the devourer for our sakes.

Our Weapons

No matter how Satan comes against us and our resources,

we have the needed weapons to defeat him. We can tithe and pray. Our obedience in tithing puts the power of the Word of God into our prayer. Disobedience always takes power out of prayer and makes us vulnerable to the enemy. All of us who represent Christ to this last-days generation are blessed to be a blessing. We must stand our ground, represent Jesus Christ, be an example, prove the Word, defeat the devourer, glorify our Father in heaven and fulfill His purpose in our lives. We are His stewards. We are more than conquerors.

There can be no denying that America's sins have set this great nation on a course to receive judgment. Some of the judgments are already obvious, and others are building rapidly. Although judgment is frightening, there are several things we should keep in mind. Judgment from God can be redemptive. It gets our attention. We begin to focus on that which is really important instead of that which amuses us. People who have no interest in God at other times often become very focused when things get serious. Many will seek God and repent during the time of judgment.

Prayer becomes popular during judgment. As the bumper sticker reminds us, "As long as students have final exams, there will be prayer in school." Not only do the sinners pray, but God's people become much more prayerful too. And it works.

God sought for one of His people to stand in the gap and make up the hedge through prayer that He might withhold His judgment (Ezekiel 22:30). You and I have influence with God. That influence can even delay judgment if we pray earnestly for it.

Judgment can prove the Word of God. As people try to understand the things judgment brings, some will turn to the Word of God. As they see the principles of the Word that have been broken and the consequences forecast by the Word, some see the connection. They begin to see into the world of spirit and truth.

The Bible also informs us that God can protect the righteous even as He delivers judgments (Ezekiel 14:19, 20). Our righteousness, however, will protect only us individually in time of judgment. Our prayers can help delay judgment. But once it comes, our own personal standing with the Lord is the only real protection. We do not have to be afraid . . . just be faithful and obedient.

Pretended Piety

It isn't unusual for us to hear very pious-sounding statements regarding stewardship. Some like to preach that there is no reward in tithing and giving. Others don't go quite as far but still say we should never tithe for material blessing. That really sounds religious, doesn't it? But what does the Bible say?

God not only challenges us to prove Him through tithing, He also says, "Your words have been stout against me" (Malachi 3:13). He rebuked the Jews for saying there is no profit in serving God. God had promised blessing for tithing. He is offended by anyone who denies His promise of blessing.

Let us never deny the Word of God in what we say and do, no matter how pious it sounds to speak contrarily. God has established His principles and declared His promises. He delights in fulfilling His truth and in blessing us.

Love for God is our highest motivation. But we only love Him because He first loved us. Even our love for Him is simply returning some of the love He gave to us.

How many farmers would plow and plant each year if they didn't have the hope of a multiplied harvest? Even so, it is all right for tithers and givers to believe God's promise of blessing. And we must never forget, we are blessed to be a blessing.

CHAPTER 11

MAKING FRIENDS WITH MONEY

A Challenging Parable

One of the most challenging portions of the teachings of Jesus is found in Luke 16. Several verses in this chapter require considerable study and thought to grasp their meaning. And all of them require the context of the rest of Scripture to assure balance in our assessment.

I am convinced that a special reward awaits every believer who will make the effort to understand difficult passages. When the Holy Spirit unfolds these truths, they seem especially refreshing. He is sent to us for that very purpose. The keys to receiving His fresh insights appear to be a worshipful attitude, a diligence to study, a prayerful heart and an obedient spirit.

Jesus told of an unjust steward. The steward had been entrusted with his master's business. He had great responsibility and authority commensurate to that responsibility. For some reason, we are not told what, the steward had become careless. That is just human nature for many of us. If left to our own devices, we tend to deteriorate in our performance.

Accountability

This steward received a shocking message from his

master. *You must give an accounting for your stewardship.* This message produced great fear in his heart. He suddenly became very focused on his situation. Apparently, he had given little or no consideration to the prospect of having to give an accounting. By disregarding this great reality and inevitability of stewardship, he had allowed himself to become careless and selfish. Just because he now had to give an accounting, he knew he was in trouble. It was not necessary for him to conduct an audit of his performance to discover how he was going to fare in the upcoming accounting to his master. He knew at once that he was in trouble. He knew he had not been faithful in the trust that had been given to him.

Jesus expects us to make the comparison to our own lives. Each of us has been given a trust. God is the owner and master. He has allowed us to take responsibility for assets which we do not own. He has given us the privilege to stand in Christ's stead and conduct the business of the Kingdom upon the earth. It is an awesome privilege.

We are confronted with the constant temptation to become careless with this great trust divinely assigned to us. Through distraction, selfishness, greed, or just plain laziness, we are liable to neglect our responsibility, or even violate the terms of the trust. When we become guilty of falling into the pattern of the unjust steward, we also become terrified in contemplation of our Master's demand that we *give an accounting* of our stewardship.

However, Satan always encourages us to indulge those fleshly tendencies that violate our stewardship. Then he gives the false comfort that the day of accounting is far in the future. We are always encouraged to disobey today because we have tomorrow to straighten up the record and prepare for the accounting. But we cannot fix things *tomorrow.* Everything we do must be done in the present tense. We cannot enter the past nor the future. We live in the now. And we can only make the necessary changes in our behavior now.

The Accuser

Someone accused the unjust steward to his master. The charge was that he had wasted his goods. Apparently, the master still trusted his steward until this incident precipitated the accounting. How very much like our lives this story is!

The world offers us continual opportunities to waste the resources entrusted to us. Never has a generation developed more ways to waste money on unneeded things and worthless activities. The Enemy provides philosophies to justify the profligate spending. And then he accuses you to your Master that you have wasted His goods.

Satan's work is only half done when he persuades us to any act of disobedience. His accusations to God against us and his accusations against us to ourselves are intended to set off feelings of guilt and depression. If we do not take these matters to God for forgiveness and correction, then the fruit of our unfaithfulness will be very bitter. The peace of mind, the joy in our hearts, even the health in our bodies will all leave us.

If we will quickly run to God each time we realize we have been unfaithful in our stewardship, if we will repent and receive His forgiveness, and if we will cooperate with God's Word in effecting the necessary changes, then our experience will be a real step of progress. God's grace is available to us for forgiveness in response to real repentance. His grace is available to change us when we are willing to cooperate with him in disciplining ourselves. And His grace will flow through us to bless others when we live in faithfulness to Him and His Word.

The Confrontation

The master called his unjust steward and reported to him what he had heard. He called for the steward to give an account, but he did leave him room to be restored. If the accounting proved the accusation to be false, he would retain his position.

Just as surely as God the Creator owns all that He has created, we are also going to give an accounting to Him. Paul reminds us of this truth very candidly in Romans 14:12 and in 2 Corinthians 5:10. Every spending, giving and managing decision we make must be against the backdrop of this certain inevitability.

The steward in our story immediately reviewed his options only to discover there weren't any good ones left. He concluded that he was guilty and the accounting would cost him his position. By his own estimate, he was not strong enough to earn his living at manual labor and he was too proud to beg. Consequently, he resolved to exercise his remaining authority in an unjust manner to obligate those with whom he conducted business for his master.

The Compromise

In the process of compromising his trust, he had also compromised himself. He had become weak physically and morally. His pride had taken over and was making ruin of his life. The solution, he thought, was to make one big step of compromise and do what he would not have considered before. Is that not the pattern Satan follows with us? By little steps of compromise he leads us to embrace the unthinkable and to do it. Now that the evil plot had been hatched, he sprang into action. He called every one of his lord's debtors and easily seduced them to participate since they were the immediate beneficiaries of his scheme. What the steward proposed was not illegal. He had the authority to deal in behalf of his master. The debtors were not implicated in any criminal action. However, it was an unjust and immoral act. That meant that if they understood what was happening, then they were compromising themselves as accessories. By accepting the plan and the financial benefit to themselves, they were becoming obligated to this steward. And that fulfilled his purpose.

The Commendation

The lord of the unjust steward commended him because he had shown wisdom in preparing for an otherwise difficult future. Yet he could not afford to have the steward any longer in his hire, because of his irresponsible management of resources and his squandering them for his own good. We sometimes admire the cunning of wicked men, but we dare not have dealings with them.

God is faced with a similar dilemma. There are thousands of men and women of great talent who cannot be used in the kingdom of God. Why? They are unfaithful. That is the one indispensable quality God requires of those who represent Him and receive His anointing: "Moreover it is required in stewards, that a man be found faithful" (1 Corinthians 4:2).

Unwise Children

Jesus then gives us one of His hard sayings: "For the children of this world are in their generation wiser than the children of light" (Luke 16:8). It is as if we who have chosen Jesus, the greatest decision we could ever make, are being unfavorably compared to those who have failed to choose Him.

We have seen it in our own lives and in the lives of others. We Christians often make poor decisions, or no decision at all. It is almost as if our eyes have been opened to eternity and now we can't get proper focus on this present life. Jesus taught us great truths regarding resources and their application in this life. He showed us how that obedience will change us and increase heaven's population, as well. But we go on living and wasting resources as if there were no eternity.

The contrast is that the children of this world may not believe in eternity, but they do make the effort to provide for their future years here. Wisdom demands that we prepare for both this life and the next. Jesus did limit the comparison by crediting the children of this world with

111

greater wisdom only in their generation or for the space of earthly life. They have shown no wisdom in the realm of eternity. Christ led us to understand that He would like for us not only to decide for Him for eternity but also to work diligently to affect eternity. Be as motivated and cunning about the spiritual opportunities here as unbelievers are in temporal things.

Our Consternation

Jesus' next statement has provoked some consternation in efforts to understand His meaning: "Make to yourselves friends of the mammon of unrighteousness; that, when ye fail, they may receive you into everlasting habitations" (v. 9).

We know that "mammon of unrighteousness" refers to material wealth and expressly to money. Believers have been redeemed, but they live in an unredeemed world. Money is unrighteous in the sense that it is issued by unrighteous governments to be used in secular pursuits. Many of those activities are to good ends, but man's goodness is not capable of producing righteousness. Paul spoke of this when he wrote to the Romans (6:20) regarding the impossibility of man's best efforts to produce righteousness.

However, Paul also reminded us that there is a way God has ordained to devote or sanctify mammon. He declares in Romans 11:16 that "if the firstfruit be holy, the lump is also holy." The first step then in following the instructions of Christ regarding the highest use of mammon is to dedicate it to God through the tithe. This bringing of the firstfruits not only sanctifies the tenth but also the entire amount. Obviously, one could tithe and then misuse the remaining 90 percent and forfeit the blessing. But this important first step ordinarily represents a heartfelt desire to follow through with a sanctified intent in the use of the entire amount.

Tithing sets the stage for giving of offerings for the glory of God. Scripture expresses that pattern: tithes *and* offerings. And it is the Old Testament example to us.

Eternal Companions

Now, regarding the making of friends by the use of money, let us look to the end of Christ's command and work back from there. "They may receive you into everlasting habitations." The unjust steward used the resources and authority entrusted to him to make friends who would receive him when his position expired. Though he acted unjustly, he was cunning and he was thinking ahead. Christ is urging us now to justly use those resources entrusted to us with an eye toward eternity.

The only way anyone can welcome us into eternal habitations is if they have experienced redemption through the gospel of Jesus Christ. For that welcome to be personal indicates that we have made an investment in the gospel which resulted in the salvation of those particular individuals. Paul dealt with that expediency when he asked these questions: How shall they be saved except they hear, how shall they hear without a preacher, and how shall the preacher go except he be sent? (see Romans 10:14, 15).

The greatest investment God has ever made is in the salvation of souls. It cost Him His only begotten Son. Our privilege as His steward is to conduct the business of God with the understanding of what is important to Him.

Establish His Covenant

In Deuteronomy 8:18 He tells us why He gave us the power to obtain wealth: ". . . that he may establish his covenant." Money does not save, only Christ can do that. But money can very effectively pay the expense of sending the gospel and discipling believers. It cost money, and somebody gave it, perhaps sacrificially, for you to be saved. That was the establishing of God's covenant in you. Now you have the privilege through your tithing and giving to participate in establishing the covenant of God in others. Corporately, we have the opportunity to establish the covenant through the church in places we will never go, winning people we will never see until we reach heaven.

Failure and Friendship

The unjust steward lost his position because of his unfaithfulness to his lord. Jesus referred to that time, "when ye fail." Because of sin it is appointed unto man once to die. Even the righteous die. Jesus referred to that inevitable day when each one of us keeps our appointment with death. The unjust steward had to let go of all the resources which had been entrusted to him. And so will you. Jesus wanted us to manage resources in anticipation of that day.

If we have made friends by investing in souls, then they will welcome us with far greater enthusiasm than the friends of the unjust steward welcomed him. We also provide for ourselves an abundant entry into everlasting habitations by the friends we win among the great cloud of witnesses. Men and women who gave their lives for the gospel have to be thrilled by your investment in souls. The Lord himself will provide an abundant entry for everyone who is faithful unto Him.

In summary, then, we tithe and give to obey the Lord. That constitutes an investment in souls who will be special friends to us when this life is ended. Because the gospel we received has been shared with them, we all have the privilege of the home Christ has gone to prepare. They will have a special and enduring welcome for us in the everlasting habitations, as we will for those who invested in us. Jesus urged us to manage financial resources from this perspective.

Proving Faithfulness

Next, Jesus let the air out of all kinds of excuses for unfaithful stewardship. "He that is faithful in that which is least is faithful also in much: and he that is unjust in the least is unjust also in much" (Luke 16:10).

A common methodology of man is to judge ourselves by our intentions and to judge others by what they actually do. When we fail in our responsibility we offer, "I intended to do it." When we are caught doing the forbidden we say, "I didn't mean to." Jesus exposed this oft-used ploy and applied it specifically to money. That was certainly appropriate since we live with the ongoing challenge of actually doing what we should with money. Everywhere we look there is an enticement to buy a pleasure, purchase a trinket, invest in another toy — unlimited opportunities to spend selfishly and foolishly. Jesus reminded us of the virtue and the imperative of faithfulness.

For many, the unfaithfulness with money begins immediately upon its acquisition. Unless we deliberately subordinate the newly acquired mammon to Jesus, unless we put the kingdom of God first in our finances, unless we declare His lordship over every increase through the tithe, then we are unfaithful in our calling as His steward. That's what Jesus is telling us.

When I experience an increase of $100, how much of that is tithe? $10, of course. How much is left after the tithe? $90. Which portion is the least? The tithe, obviously. And what did Jesus say about me and the least portion? "He that is faithful in that which is least is faithful also in much."

A common excuse goes like this: "I don't actually designate what I give as tithe, but you can be sure that I always give 10 percent or more, so in that sense I am a tither," which, being interpreted, means: "I do what I want to with my money. But when I go to church, I want to be regarded as a tither, so hear my words and don't pay any attention to what I do. God and I have our own thing going, and none of those old-fashioned requirements apply to me."

Accounting and Tithing

We could gather from all this that he actually intends to tithe but isn't willing to pay the price of faithfulness. A major principle in this parable is that we must give an account. One of the inherent blessings in tithing is that it gives the worshiper an opportunity to "take inventory" of his possessions and give an accounting to God every time he receives an increase. The act of tithing does not consist of simply evaluating the increase. It is also the opportunity for me to evaluate my spiritual condition on a regular basis. If my heart begins to grow cool toward God, then I will feel resistance in my heart regarding the scriptural mandate to bring the first tenth to God. That is an early warning for me to get on my knees before God in full repentance.

The punctual accounting unto God by calculating the tithe on every increase and the prompt bringing of the tithes unto Him in worship has great benefits. It keeps me from carelessness in my accounting as a steward. And it keeps me aware of the condition of my heart regarding my relationship to God as well as my relationship to mammon.

"He that is unjust in the least is unjust also in much." Jesus purposefully took away every leaf of every excuse with this powerful revelation of how He judges our stewardship unto Him. He declared with no uncertainty that the individual who does not obey His word regarding the tithe — the least portion of every increase — then that person cannot be faithful in the rest of his trust.

If I am violating my relationship with God then I cannot have a proper relationship with anyone else. If my love of money hinders my obedience to God with the first tenth, then I cannot have a proper relationship with money and possessions at all.

Another Consequence

To ensure that we not miss the point, Jesus followed the revelation of His stewardship judgment principle with a question that draws our attention to the consequences of unfaithfulness. "If therefore ye have not been faithful in the unrighteous mammon, who will commit to your trust the true riches?" (v. 11).

Some believers beg God to trust them with true riches, and wonder why their prayers go unanswered. The answer is that they are not faithful with the tithe. Therefore they are disqualified for any higher trust.

It is almost shocking. Jesus has declared that the *test* of our spiritual walk is measured by our stewardship. You see, I can talk about how much I love my wife; but if I withhold due benevolence to her, no one will believe me. Millions of people talk about loving God, but they have no evidence of that love when it comes to their finances. In fact, their love for money is far more apparent than their love for God. Any of us can pretend piety. The truth of our spiritual condition is always revealed in our attitude toward possessions.

You can tell a good deal about a person by reading his checkbook. The amounts, the frequency of distribution, and the entities which receive those moneys will give you a very accurate description of the owner of the checkbook. Jesus lets us know that God knows everything about us, and our obedience in finances is the daily test of our spirituality. The good news is that faithfulness as God's steward does qualify us for the true riches as well as an ever-growing capacity to manage mammon for Him.

Christ added one other facet to the money test in verse 12: "And if ye have not been faithful in that which is another man's, who shall give you that which is your own?" There are some obvious applications of this question. If I take advantage of my employer in not giving to him eight hours of work for eight hours of pay, I disqualify myself for greater trust in the eyes of God. But the specific subject matter calls us to task again regarding the tithe and our stewardship trust to God.

The tithe was designated to support God's ministers, from Melchizedek and the Levitical priesthood through the fivefold ministry of the New Testament (Ephesians 4:11). Anytime I am unfaithful in the tithe, I have not only affronted the priesthood of Christ, I have also taken that which is another man's, simply because God has designated that the tithe given to Him is to be used to support the minister of the gospel.

117

Context of The Parables

Finally, let us see the gravity of the teaching on the unjust steward by context. Luke 15 ends with Jesus' teaching on the Prodigal Son. He was restored to his position as a son in the house of his father, but he had lost everything material through his unfaithfulness. Verse 31 reveals that all the father's wealth would now go to his faithful son. The younger son who had been unfaithful had no possessions left.

Following the story of the unjust steward, Jesus told of another unfaithful steward and his end. The certain rich man who squandered riches on himself but could show no compassion for Lazarus died and went to hell. Can you go to hell for unfaithful stewardship? The one sin that takes anyone to hell is rejecting Christ. What we do with money shows whether we are rejecting Him or not.

The Prodigal Son repented. He was restored, but without his posssessions. There is a price to pay for leaving God. The rich man never repented. He was forever lost. God gives us the opportunity to grow and be rewarded in this life and the next for faithful stewardship. Because He examines us by our faithfulness to tithe, to give and to obey, it is entirely appropriate for us to "give an account" of every increase and return the first tenth promptly to Him as a celebration of His lordship.

TITHING
IN THE
NEW TESTAMENT

Pertinent Questions

Was the practice of tithing carried over into the New Testament? Opponents declare it was not. However, they have not one verse of Scripture upon which to base their assertion. Since there is no Scripture to authorize their specious claim, they usually resort to a fall-back position and claim that the New Testament is silent on tithing. When we have demonstrated that to be untrue, then we will have the authority of the Word to guide us in this foundational aspect of Christian stewardship.

The questions we will wish to answer are

1. What is the testimony of New Testament Scripture?

2. Is the lordship of Christ concerning our possessions still important?

3. Do we need the blessing that accompanies tithing as we endeavor to obey the New Testament?

4. Is there a better way to disciple believers and support the work of the church?

In my own experience I have observed that those individuals who have difficulty finding tithing in the New Testament usually have a similar difficulty in locating Christ in the Old Testament. The early church did not have a written

New Testament. It was necessary for them to always present Christ from the Old Testament, and they did it very effectively. In this study we will not explore every New Testament verse that touches on tithing, but we will review a sufficient number to satisfy the sincere believer.

Jesus taught in Matthew 6 that we were not to make the pursuit of things our major objective in life. That is the lifestyle of the heathen. "But seek ye first the kingdom of God, and his righteousness; and all these things shall be added unto you" (Matthew 6:33). The people to whom Jesus spoke were familiar with the Scriptures. They knew the provision for putting God first in material things was the tithe. And they knew that putting God first would bring blessing—"all these things shall be added unto you."

Christ's instruction to seek first the Kingdom includes more than material things and more than tithe. But it certainly embraces the concept of tithing. If not, these listeners would have been greatly frustrated, and so would we. Their Scripture had provided no other way to put God "first" in possessions, and neither does the New Testament.

As the apostle Paul stated, the Old Testament was a schoolmaster to bring us to Christ. That is such an appropriate analogy. School is a common experience to us all. After spending so many years learning necessary principles for the relationships of life, how foolish we would be to abandon them. And how difficult is life for that one who refuses to use the tools provided.

Could a Christian be so foolish as to set aside the only scriptural provision for putting the kingdom of God first in the realm of possessions? That would be an attitude of rebellion. To disregard Scripture is to dishonor God. To abandon the truths taught us by a worthy schoolmaster would be folly. To fail God's instruction is robbery.

Millions of Christians have proved the truth and the promise of Christ's teaching by seeking first the kingdom of God through faithful tithing. You may prove this truth with your own life. As you do, you will glorify God, edify the church and experience a wonderful fulfillment for yourself.

Wrongfully Tithing

I met a man in Hurst, Texas, who shared his testimony with me. He grew up in a church that did not believe in tithing. They actually taught their people that it was a sin to tithe. As he matured spiritually, he began to recognize some of the doctrinal errors of his church from his own study of the Word. He began to search for a more scripturally balanced congregation.

When he found a church he liked, he was appalled to hear them encourage people to tithe. He had never studied the subject. He simply accepted what he had been told, so this seemed awful to him to hear the pastor encouraging people to tithe.

Because he liked everything else they had to say about the Word, and he liked their worship and fellowship, he delayed leaving. When the 1981 recession came, his business really went into severe decline. Because he supplied oil-drilling equipment and the oil industry was diminishing daily, it occurred to him that this was the opportunity for a personal test which would help these good people get a proper understanding about tithing. He would tithe just to prove there is no blessing in it. And so he began. To his astonishment, his business stopped its decline. Week by week it showed marked increases. The oil industry continued in its downward fall. He had done nothing different except to tithe. Instead of proving that it was wrong to tithe, he had inadvertently proved God's promise to be true. He had demonstrated the power of the Word through his obedience to it. He was a witness to God's faithfulness to His Word.

This experience opened his mind and heart to the scriptures on tithing. As he increased in understanding, he became excited about sharing his experience with others. Now his life serves to prove God's Word through faithful stewardship. Every believer is entitled to the same privilege through the same principles and promises to faithful stewards.

Idolatry

The opposite story can also be told. Many have proved

the Word of God through disobedience. We can seek first the "things" and lose the Kingdom. Idolatry is a cruel religion at all times. Throughout history, when idolatry became strong enough, it called for human sacrifice. Lives were wasted to satisfy the lust of demons. Idolatry has risen to great power again and is demanding the blood of humans. Abortion is nothing less than raging idolatry. It will continue to increase and eventually claim the lives of other groups unless the church repents and asserts its spiritual authority to restrain it.

The consequences of materialism are grave indeed. When Christians took lightly God's command to put Him first, when the church began to back away from the scriptural charge to tithe, few believed the spiritual decline would come so fast and so large. Bringing possessions under the lordship of Christ is important. Tithing is a powerful defense against materialism. It is a wonderful protection against idolatry.

Unto God the Things That Are God's

The life of Jesus is a tremendous enjoyment for those who love good debate. Pharisees, Saducees and lawyers sought desperately for a way to entrap Him. They came up with some pretty impressive schemes . . . until Jesus exposed them.

In Matthew 22:15-22 the Pharisees launched another attempt to entrap Jesus. They sent their disciples with the Herodians to confront Jesus. This way there would be witnesses against Him either way He responded to their questions.

They began with flattery that was expected to disarm Christ and His followers. "'Is it lawful to give tribute unto Caesar, or not?'" A "yes" answer should alienate all of the Jews who resented Roman rule. A "no" answer would validate a charge of rebellion against the ruling government. They had Him for sure, they thought.

Jesus perceived their wickedness and asked, "Why tempt ye me, ye hypocrites? Shew me the tribute money." And they brought to Him a penny. He asked a second question:

"Whose is this image and superscription?" They answered, "Caesar's" Jesus said to them, "Render therefore unto Caesar the things which are Caesar's; and unto God the things that are God's." When they heard His words, they were amazed and left Him and went their way.

This was truly great drama—the Pharisees and Herodians were pretending to admire Jesus to set the stage for their strategic question. Their only purpose in asking was an effort to destroy Him. Jesus so easily set aside their hypocrisy. He called them hypocrites. They had tried to disarm Him with flattery; He disarmed them with truth.

Then He used them to display the truth. Their tax money carried the mark of the emperor. Caesar had minted the money. It belonged to him as creator of it. Of course, he could tax it. Once those truths were put on display, they had no standing to argue further before this crowd.

But Jesus wasn't through with them. He chose this opportunity to deal with the greater truth of tithing also. Whose image is upon us? God's image. What does that mean? It means He is absolute owner. Who created all that is? God did. Then does He have the right to call for us to submit ourselves to Him? And to bring to Him the tithe? More surely than Caesar's right to tax the money he created, God has the right to call for the tithe from us.

The Jews immediately remembered from Scripture that God had proclaimed, "And all the tithe of the land, whether of the seed of the land, or of the fruit of the tree, is the Lord's: it is holy unto the Lord" (Leviticus 27:30). Nowhere has God instructed us that He has changed His mind. Jesus instructed the challengers, His followers and us to pay both taxes and tithes.

The context was money. The decision was definite. The command was clear: render. The dictionary defines that word "to give back." Give back to Caesar that which belongs to him. Give back to God that which belongs to Him. Caesar claimed the tax. God claims the tithe. The command is to us as well.

Jesus' Confirmation of the Tithe

In Matthew 23 Jesus exposed a number of religious hypocrisies. He spoke of leaders who don't obey the teachings they require of others. Phony display of piety and the constant pursuit of honor were judged by Christ: "Whosoever shall exalt himself shall be abased" (v. 12). He accused, "Ye devour widows' houses, and for a pretence make long prayer" and indicated they would "receive the greater damnation" (v. 14). He dealt with deceitful swearing, calling them blind fools for doing it. Then He gave them perspective on tithing.

Some of the Jews were so precise about tithing they would even tithe the spices in their kitchens (v. 23). Yet Jesus called them hypocrites because they were meticulous about tithing but omitted the weightier matters of the law. He made it clear that tithing is not a substitute for other Christian virtues. He called judgment, mercy and faith weightier matters than tithing. Jesus helped us to have perspective on tithing so that we would not substitute it for other things.

Then Christ confirmed the practice of tithing. "These ought ye to have done, and not to leave the other undone" (v. 23). He told them they ought to practice judgment, mercy and faith. But He also made it clear that they were not to leave tithing undone.

Is the New Testament believer still responsible to practice judgment, mercy and faith? Who would deny it under any pretext? Then honor the words of our Lord. Don't leave tithing undone in your life. He is Lord, and He rewards obedience and punishes disobedience.

Did Jesus Tithe?

Have you ever pondered that question? Did Jesus tithe while He was on the earth? Although the Scriptures do not speak directly to that question, they do provide sufficient evidence for us to reach a conclusion.

When Jesus came to John for water baptism, John forbade Him, saying, "I have need to be baptized of thee, and comest thou to me?" Jesus answered, "Suffer it to be so now: for thus it becometh us to fulfil all righteousness" (Matthew 3:14, 15). We can see by this encounter and their conversation that Jesus was committed to satisfy all the demands of Scripture. That would certainly include tithing.

Another evidence is that Jesus' instruction concerning tithing, some of which we have just reviewed, would leave Him in an untenable position if He did not practice what He preached. He would never be hypocritical. One of the things He greatly despised was hypocrisy. Certainly He did fulfill all righteousness, and He was not a hypocrite. Therefore, we may conclude He tithed.

It is most interesting also that although the Pharisees accused Him of anything they thought someone might be persuaded to believe, they never accused Him of failure to tithe. Evidently even His worst enemies didn't expect anyone would believe such a slander.

The principle of tithing was embraced by the law under Moses. And it was embraced by grace under Jesus Christ.

Matthew closed his book by quoting Jesus' final command to us. We call it the Great Commission (Matthew 28:19, 20). In verse 19 He commands us to evangelize the people of the world. In verse 20 He commanded us to disciple them: "Teaching them to observe all things whatsoever I have commanded you." That includes (1) rendering to God the things that are God's and (2) doing the things we ought to do and not leaving the other (tithing) undone. Thus, He has instructed us to tithe and to teach those who come to Christ to tithe also.

Why the Confusion?

Jesus taught in parables. They were fascinating stories He used to illustrate and impart spiritual truth. He also used parables to conceal spiritual truth from those whose attitudes toward Him were wrong. The disciples asked Him why He used parables, and He explained: "Unto you it is given to know the mystery of the kingdom of God: but unto them that are without, all these things are done in parables: that seeing they may see, and not perceive; and hearing they may hear, and not understand; lest at any time they should be converted, and their sins should be forgiven them" (Mark 4:11, 12).

He then continued to fully explain the parable of the sower. "The sower soweth the word. And these are they by the way side . . . but when they have heard, Satan cometh immediately, and taketh away the word that was sown in their hearts" (Mark 4:14, 15). Some are confused simply because Satan has stolen the Word from them. They never understand tithing, or other teachings, because the Word is not in their hearts. They may have the Word in their heads, but Jesus taught that it must be in our hearts.

We can keep the Word in our hearts only by an attitude of submissiveness to Christ and His Word. Any rebellion toward God or His Word gives Satan the opportunity to steal the Word from us. Rebellion leaves the heart as hard as unplowed ground. The seed cannot penetrate.

Jesus described another wrong condition, which He likened to stony ground. Those people respond to the Word and "immediately receive it with gladness; and have no root in themselves, and so endure but for a time: afterward when affliction or persecution ariseth for the word's sake, immediately they are offended" (Mark 4:16, 17). This group is defeated over tithing or any other scriptural truth by the first affliction or persecution that comes their way. Every spiritual battle is over the Word of God. All of God's people go through times of attack. Winners refuse to stop their practice of the Word.

Jesus described a third condition: "They which are sown among thorns; such as hear the word, and the cares of this world, and the deceitfulness of riches, and the lusts of other things entering in, choke the word, and it becometh unfruitful" (Mark 4:18, 19). Jesus dealt with the answer to "the cares of this world" when He taught us to seek first the kingdom of God. If we put the temporary ahead of the eternal in our priorities, we will be victimized by the cares of this life, we will lose our peace of mind, and the Word will be choked so that it cannot bear fruit in us.

The deceitfulness of riches is one of Satan's most success-ful ploys. This device works extremely well on large numbers of people all over the world. People are led to believe that money will solve all their problems and give them happiness too. Even Christians are subjected to the influence of this false belief through a deceived society, mass media propaganda and confused believers.

The practice of tithing shines the light of truth into the darkness of deception and helps us to keep our lives properly ordered. Satan will have a difficult time deceiving us if we stand by God's Word and subordinate every possession to the lordship of Jesus through faithful tithing.

"Lusts of other things" is the third negative step in this downward progression and constitutes idolatry. At this point the victim has fallen down to worship Satan. The Word of God has been rendered unfruitful in this person's life.

But Jesus described a fourth type of hearers of the Word—those who are sown on good ground. They hear the Word, they receive it, and they bear fruit abundantly (Mark 4:20). They are not confused about God's Word. They hear it gladly. And they receive it in an open, obedient and worship-ing heart. They do not release their hold on the Word. They bear fruit. They are faithful disciples. They tithe all of their increase. They glorify God. And they are fulfilled.

Understanding Through Commitment

Confusion concerning tithing then comes from ignorance of God's Word, resistance to God's Word, shallow commit-ment to the Word, covetousness and false teaching about the Word. God has promised that we will find Him when we put Him first in our lives (Deuteronomy 4:29). But until we make that genuine commitment to Him, we will not understand His Word. Jesus said to those who had forsaken all to follow Him, "Unto you it is given to know the mystery of the kingdom of God" (Mark 4:11). Then He explained that His message was designed to prevent understanding by those uncommitted.

One of the saddest portions in Scripture was written to us by John. He provided additional insight from the teaching of Jesus concerning this problem of commitment. "Now when he was in Jerusalem at the passover, in the feast day, many believed in his name, when they saw the miracles which he did. But Jesus did not commit himself unto them, because he knew all men, and needed not that any should testify of man: for he knew what was in man" (John 2:23-25). He could see into their hearts. Because they had no commitment to Him, they would receive no commitment from Him. That meant they would never enjoy having the Word of God opened to their hearts by the Holy Spirit. For lack of commitment to Him they would always lack relationship and understanding.

Churches today have people with the same problem. There are thousands who claim they believe in his name. They call themselves Christians. They attempt to use His name. But they are not committed to Him. He looks on our hearts. He knows what is in us. He cannot be fooled. Therefore, He is not committed to the uncommitted.

When we seek the kingdom of God first, when we seek Him with all of our hearts, when we have forsaken all to follow Him . . . He knows it. And He commits Himself to us. His covenant commitments become very real to us. We enjoy the security of relationship with Him. And it shows up in every aspect of our living. It appears in our finances as a tithe to Him. If He isn't first in our money, He isn't first in our lives.

Our stewardship reveals outwardly what is taking place inwardly. Tithing demonstrates materially where we are spiritually. Not only can Christ see into my heart, I can too. If I am unwilling to give Him first place over possessions, it is easy for me to see that I have not given Him the throne of my heart.

The world scoffs at Christians who say they believe in Christ but have no change in lifestyle. Sinners have good cause to be skeptical, knowing that they give their gods higher priority than many professing Christians give to Christ.

CHAPTER 13

CONFESSION
WITHOUT
CHANGE

Unchristians

Time magazine dubbed 1976 the Year of the Evangelical, declaring that more than 50 million Americans claimed to have been "born again." Later when the IRS reported the totals for giving in America, it revealed that this great growth in numbers of Christians hadn't affected their pocketbooks.

The born-again revival didn't mean much if our values were unchanged. To be sure, many of those claiming born-again status didn't even know what it meant. And some of the churches they happened into didn't know either. It was popular to be born again . . . and it didn't cost anything.

Many of them would have become disciples if given the opportunity. They would have practiced scriptural stewardship had they been taught the Scriptures. Compromised and compromising clergy were afraid these newcomers would abandon the church if they were told what Christ expected of them. Instead of losing them *from* the church, they lost them *in* the church.

After that it made little difference whether they stayed or not. Gradually they sensed that it made little difference and either drifted along or drifted away. Clergy who compromise the Word soon compromise the congregation. A compromised church leads to a compromised community . . . and eventually to a comprised nation. Who would have believed that failure to teach believers to tithe and give could bring down a nation? Israel.

What would have happened if recent converts had been told that Jesus said, "Whosoever he be of you that forsaketh not all that he hath, he cannot be my disciple" (Luke 14:33)? Yes, some would have left. But those who remained would have grown strong in the faith. They would have matured in Christ. They would have become spiritually productive. The church would have grown to win and disciple others. The purpose of God would be carried out. He would be glorified.

When the cares of this world, the deceitfulness of riches and the lusts of other things choke the Word of God in the church, that church becomes unfruitful and a generation of people is cut off from the truth. The church has no right to exist apart from preaching, teaching and practicing the Word. If a church fails here, it is wasting resources . . . spiritual and material.

Out of the Heart

When Jesus looked into men's hearts, what did He see? Fortunately, He told us in Mark 7:21, 22. Among the 13 evil, defiling things that come out of man's heart, two deal directly with stewardship: thefts and covetousness. To steal declares that we do not trust God to supply our need as He has promised or that we are not satisfied with His provision and are envious of the provision to others. Covetousness says we desire some portion of the creation more than we desire relationship with the Creator. Remember, covetousness is idolatry.

Repentance is turning to God for forgiveness and deliverance from all these defilements. Stewardship is practicing the lordship of Christ so that the scriptural priorities remain in my heart. Tithing protects me from stealing from God. It testifies that He is my source and my security. It shows that I look to the Creator and not to what He has created. When God is first, then I will have no other gods before Him. There will be no

130

idolatry in my heart when God is first. The firstfruits of all the increase will verify His lordship in my life. Jesus did not reveal problems and just leave us to worry with them. He told us how to enjoy solutions through Him. "Whosoever will come after me, let him deny himself, and take up his cross, and follow me" (Mark 8:34). We are required to deny self. It is almost irresistible to make self the center of life. We all declare a dislike for self-centered people, but that is the most common centering for every one of us. Yet we are created beings—greatly inferior to the Creator. To center on self is just another form of idolatry. Jesus said He will set us free from this idol also.

Deny yourself. To deny myself means I am no longer first in my own living. The removal of self from my heart leaves a vacuum. I must reserve the throne of my heart for Jesus. If He is first, I will manifest it materially by tithing. If I refuse to tithe, I have put myself first again. He said that He must be first (Matthew 22:37).

Take up your cross. He means carry the cross. What is it for? Dying. After He has saved me, my spirit is born again, but I continue my earthly life in unredeemed flesh. The world, the flesh and the devil give me problems. But if I always have that cross handy, I can crucify the flesh every time it resists the rule of Christ.

Follow Me. Jesus always put God first . . . in His prayers, work, giving and dying. His invitation is a command. A little child can follow. Yet a learned theologian can never exhaust the challenge of the Lord's exciting opportunity to follow Him. We can follow Him only if He is first . . . in everything.

Romans and Tithing

We have already referred to the apostle Paul's gracious reminder of a tithing principle in Romans 11:16. He did not want us to forget that tithing sanctifies material things so we are satisfied stewards instead of miserable materialists.

He became more direct in his message in Romans 13:7. "Render therefore to all their dues: tribute to whom tribute is due; custom to whom custom; fear to whom fear; honour to whom honour." In consideration of the instruction to "render to all their dues," he reminded us as Christ did to "render . . . unto Caesar [taxes]" and "[render] unto God [tithes]" (Matthew 22:21). Christ also taught us that God is to be first whether we are rendering, fearing or honoring (Matthew 6:33; 22:37).

"The fear of the Lord is the beginning of wisdom" (Psalm 111:10). One of the ways we show a proper fear of the Lord is through obedience or faithfulness. The steward who fears the Lord will receive commendation at the time of accounting (Matthew 25:21).

Honor is due to God. Before Malachi gave us his great teaching on tithing, he asked the Lord's question: "A son honoureth his father, and a servant his master: if then I be a father, where is mine honour?" (Malachi 1:6). Solomon said, "Honour the Lord with thy substance, and with the firstfruits of all thine increase" (Proverbs 3:9). Paul's command to honor the Lord has specific meaning because of these scriptural precedents.

We are also faced with these difficult challenges: How can we render unto the Lord, how can we fear Him, how can we honor Him without obedience to His instructions concerning tithing, giving and managing all that He entrusts to us? The Scriptures provide no alternative.

The Soul Exchange

Jesus reminded us of the magnitude of our response. Some have never invested in the stock market, but most know of the great stock exchanges where the enterprises and resources of the world are bought and sold. Jesus spoke of a far greater trading center . . . the soul exchange. Everyone will invest here whether the market is up or down. And we will spend everything we have in the soul exchange.

Jesus understood profits; He invested in the world. The Creator spent Himself to buy back His creation . . . that investment was made for us. Now it is our turn to invest. So He asked the question, "For what shall it profit a man, if he shall gain the whole world, and lose his own soul? Or what shall a man give in exchange for his soul?" (Mark 8:36, 37).

Is it possible to lose our soul over things? Jesus said it is. Stewardship is serious business. Tithing carries a significance of great magnitude. It is not just an investment for blessing. It also communicates and establishes our priorities. It may well reveal where we are in the soul exchange. It is our first line of defense against materialism. It not only positions God first in my life materially, it also places Jesus first ahead of me. By this act I make a first step of denying self upon the receipt of every increase.

Does all this mean that if I tithe I cannot lose in the soul exchange? No, it doesn't mean that. Jesus said we must fulfill the weightier matters also. Tithing is an important step, but it is not a substitute for the other steps in following Christ. It is a first step financially, but if other steps are not taken, if the relationship is not respected and developed, then we still place ourselves at risk.

The rich young ruler (Mark 10:17-22) illustrated the problem for us. He was a faithful Jew. He testified of his faithfulness to follow the commandments of the law. He was a tither. He confirmed that he did not steal. Jesus loved him . . . and looked into his heart. He saw that he had shifted his trust from God, the Creator, to wealth, the creation.

Jesus gave him the same opportunity for deliverance and salvation that He offers us: "Sell everything (deny self) give it to the poor, take up your cross, and follow Me." But the young man wouldn't do it. He trusted in his riches. He had become an idolater in his heart. Jesus asked him to give up his god, to change from an earthly, temporal focus to a heavenly, eternal one.

Although he had been blessed for tithing, he didn't take the other steps. He lost out spiritually. His encounter with Jesus turned from opportunity to exposure. He went away sad and grieving. Here was a tither who discovered what his own soul was selling for on the soul exchange. Tithing is not salvation. It is a response to it. It is a testimony, a protection, a change of focus, a means of blessing. Tithing declares the lordship of Jesus in my life only if I have made Him Lord.

Friends of Mammon

We cannot serve God and mammon (Luke 16:13). Jesus explained that if we love riches, we will hate God. We will hold to one and despise the other. None of us can serve two masters. When Saul met Christ on the road to Damascus, he learned to love God and count all material things as dung. He was freed from materialism by his relationship with the Creator.

The Bible calls material possessions by some negative terms. Money is referred to as filthy lucre and unrighteous mammon.

Every believer would have serious conflict here if not for the tithe. It would be extremely inconvenient for me if I were forbidden to make use of money. Money is one of man's greatest inventions, but it is definitely part of the fallen, unredeemed, material world. Nevertheless, when I bring to God the firstfruits of all that He has entrusted to me, that which remains is no longer filthy lucre. Tithing has made it holy. When I give the tithe to the Lord, I no longer have unrighteous mammon in my bank account. Tithing has sanctified the entire amount unto the lordship of Christ.

Diabolical Distortion

Jesus' teaching on two masters calls our attention to the original distortion of God's purpose. He created us for the high calling of relationship with Him. He provided for us to be in His image and likeness. Through conformity to Christ and the opportunity to know His will, along with the discipline of following it, we thereby grow toward maturity in Christ. Sin allowed a created being (Satan) to take God's place of influence. Our misuse of creation declared that man viewed the material realm as being of more value than the Creator who made it. That distortion is demeaning to man. It is rebellion against God. It exalts God's ugly enemy.

Paul reminded us that tithing is the practice which helps to restore divine order. Tithing acknowledges God as first, Christ as preeminent, Satan as deceiver, and money as a tool to be used for good in the hand of the believer.

An adage says, "Money is a good servant but a cruel master." Jesus admonished us not to permit money to become our master. When God is first in our lives, money will be a servant to us. Through our obedience, money entrusted to us will be sanctified and will accomplish much good.

Should we choose to disobey, we will see money become master over us. It will become our god. Sometimes too late men discover with horror that if we serve money, we worship Satan . . . and receive with him God's final judgment. It is serious business.

Tithing is a great blessing to us because it helps to break the deception of Satan and riches. It restores true order and proper perspective in the life of the believer. It maintains that perspective of truth. It is a basis for God's protection. It is a principle of true prosperity.

The Test

Jesus said, "If therefore ye have not been faithful in the unrighteous mammon, who will commit to your trust the true riches?" (Luke 16:11). Money is a testing ground. God is looking for faithfulness. Paul repeated this truth when he said, "Moreover it is required in stewards, that a man be found faithful" (1 Corinthians 4:2).

What is faithfulness? Diligent compliance with the owner's instructions. In other words, whatever God says . . . do it. This is where Adam failed. He was unfaithful in managing God's property according to God's Word. That's the same problem with most people today.

Why is faithfulness so important? Only through faithfulness can God's purpose be realized in us. After we are born in His image, we begin the process of growing up "unto the measure of the stature of the fulness of Christ" (Ephesians 4:13). That growth is based upon knowing Him, knowing His

Word, speaking His Word and doing His Word. Faithfulness to Him and His Word is absolutely essential if we are to be conformed to Him. Through faithfulness, God's purpose of revealing Himself in us is attained.

Jesus said we must show faithfulness in money. The first step in the test is the tithe. If I fail to obey Him on this point, I have interrupted the divine process. I will have denied His lordship. I will have compromised myself through robbery. I will have disqualified myself for true riches. I will have failed the test at the beginning if I decline to tithe.

But through obedience, God is glorified, my life is kept in true perspective, I am being conformed to Him, I am protected and blessed, and I pass the first test of stewardship.

What kind of response did Jesus receive from this teaching? Essentially the same one He gets today: "And the Pharisees also, who were covetous, heard all these things: and they derided him" (Luke 16:14). Covetous people still disobey Him and deride Him for His teaching on tithing and giving.

But we all have the privilege of faithful cooperation. That's when God works His wonderful purpose in us. There is no greater fulfillment available to man than to see the realization of God's purpose in us. That produces a life abounding in the fruit of the spirit. Faithfulness produces fruit. Fruit glorifies God and attracts men to Christ.

Whose Child Are You?

The Jews took great pride in being the children of Abraham. They had a right to delight in the miraculous birth of Isaac during the old age of Abraham and Sarah, which fulfilled God's promise. They were also a part of God's commitment to Abraham. But they had a bad habit of taking pride in their kinship to Abraham through the flesh and not after the Spirit.

Jesus challenged them by observing that if they were truly the children of Abraham, then they would do the works of Abraham (John 8:39). He acknowledged that they were seed of Abraham after the flesh (v. 37). But He proved that they were not seed of Abraham after the Spirit. "If ye were Abraham's children, ye would do the works of Abraham" (v. 39).

It is not uncommon for us Christians to take the same kind of pride in our relationship to Abraham. Paul told us that if we are born again by faith, then we are children of Abraham (Galatians 3:7). If we are Christ's, then we are Abraham's seed (v. 29). We have a right to be pleased that we are in the spiritual family of Abraham. He is father of the Jews and the Christians.

Jesus' challenge still stands. If we are a child of Abraham, we will do the works of Abraham. What were His works?

One of the prominent ones was tithing. According to Jesus, if we are a child of Abraham, we will tithe.

The First Church and Tithing

After the resurrection of Christ, the Day of Pentecost saw the church burst forth with a great harvest of 3,000 souls. Shortly thereafter 5,000 more were saved. The next time a count was taken, the newborn were reported as multitudes . . . too many to number. Can you imagine the cost to provide ministry and discipling for such an exploding church?

God had a plan to put into place. He moved upon the people to give everything they owned to this church, and most of them did. We believe God owns everything. Therefore, He is just in calling for all the resources He has entrusted to us at any time it pleases Him.

This was a time of unusual need because of the phenomenal growth of the church. God had long before revealed that the reason we have the power to get wealth is to facilitate the establishing of His covenant in the earth (Deuteronomy 8:18). These Christians had the unique opportunity and responsibility to fund the mother church of the Christian faith. They sponsored evangelism, discipleship and works of charity.

Christ had already prophesied of the destruction of

Jerusalem. All their possessions were going to be wrenched from them eventually, or they could give them to the Lord now and have treasure in heaven for all eternity. By releasing their possessions they not only funded the growth of the church, they also freed themselves to leave during the persecution of the church (Acts 8:1).

Now to the question: Did they practice tithing? Absolutely. When a believer brings everything to God, the tithe is included. The first tenth is still a tithe. They not only testified that God owned all, they demonstrated it, unflinchingly. What a contrast! Today some give lip service that God owns it all and then walk away with all that He has entrusted to them still in their possession.

Did Christ go to Calvary so that practicing thieves and robbers could enter heaven claiming grace as a license to steal? Certainly not. Jesus said our righteousness must exceed the Pharisees', and most of them tithed. Grace has been made available to give us strength to do what is right, not as an indulgence to disobedience, rebellion and sin.

Another question is answered in Acts 5. How important is accuracy in reporting the tithe? Ananias and Sapphira wanted to receive credit in the eyes of the church that they too were giving everything. They didn't intend to give everything. They held back part of it but affirmed to Peter that they were doing like the others. They lied. And they died.

Many today want credit for tithing in the eyes of the church. They bring some amount but not the tenth. They call it the tithe, but it isn't. One pastor warned that God may reduce a person's income accordingly. Actually, it is much more serious than that. It is lying to the Holy Spirit and can cost the offender his life.

Our Schoolmaster

The Old Testament provided a schoolmaster's blessing to us. The New Testament writers appropriately reached back for this valuable instruction and freely expressed the underlying principles in current terms. Of course, we need the principles and the understanding to make their application profitable for us and our generation.

Paul's instruction to the Corinthians is such an instance. He referred to the well-established Old Testament practice of supporting the priesthood by those things brought to the Lord as acts of worship. The instructors were quite precise, and the great number of references verified the practice beyond dispute. The Book of Psalms reveals the joy experienced by the worshipers as they gave. They understood that their offerings would be used to support the priests and Levites, yet they were giving them to God.

It seems strange that believers today are so often ignorant of the principle and the process of honoring the Lord with our substance. Many of the principles practiced before Christ came were not revealed so openly and fully for them as they have been for us through Christ. Mysteries were shielded in the Old Testament but uncovered for us. Truth was enfolded in the Old Testament and unfolded in the New. We have the most astounding opportunity to understand great truths. One of the major hurdles has been failure to teach the Word boldly. Since understanding comes through obedience, ignorance of the Word hinders its practice and blocks the opportunity to understand beautiful truths.

The Lord Ordained

Paul gave us the powerful assurance that the principles of tithing and giving which supported the priesthood are to support the ministry of the gospel. He left no room for equivocation. Look at his words: "Do ye not know that they which minister about holy things live of the things of the temple? and they which wait at the altar are partakers with the altar? Even so hath the Lord ordained that they which preach the gospel should live of the gospel" (1 Corinthians 9:13, 14).

You see how Paul brought the principles to apply without conflicting the fulfillment made by Christ. Obviously, he did not intend for us to continue with blood sacrifice. That was fulfilled by Christ at Calvary once and for all. But the underlying principles of worship through tithing and giving must not be abandoned, for they are to continue to support the ministry.

Here is the key phrase: "Even so hath the Lord ordained." "Even so" is like the equal sign in a mathematical equation. It tells us that one side of the equation matches the other. They are even. They are in balance. To eliminate or diminish tithing or giving distorts the balance.

God has given the church enough resources to fulfill the Great Commission easily. The imbalance which exists between great opportunities for the gospel and insufficient funds to man those opportunities is matched by the disobedience of believers in tithing and giving.

One student of the problem has declared that Evangelicals put enough money into their retirement programs every five years to evangelize the whole world three times. That is not to say their plans for retirement are wrong, unless they are funding them with their tithes and offerings or through some other form of disobedience. If retirement has priority over God, there exists a problem of no small dimension.

Paul assured us that the practice of these principles in Christianity is not a suggestion of his nor a good idea of others. The Lord himself ordained it. Rebellion against following this practice is rebellion against the Savior, the Lord of the church. There is no higher authority.

Channels

We are blessed to be a blessing. God did not intend for us to be reservoirs but channels. He is to be our source at all times. When we disobey Him in the use of things, we bring unfruitfulness to our lives and spiritual death follows. Through obedience we participate in, and cooperate with, what God is doing in us and in the world through us. We are blessed (1) by fulfillment of the relationship with God and (2) to see the resulting growth accomplished in us so that He may increase His use of us.

The most exciting thing in this world is the work of

Christ to build God's forever family. He invited us to be a part of the family through salvation. Through scriptural stewardship He invited you to be part of the family business. Thousands of Christians are discovering the delight and fulfillment of being one of the King's stewards. As we live through these last days and participate in the end-time harvest, God will use more men and women to facilitate ministry than ever before. The resources He is pouring through faithful stewards is amazing. Equally astounding is the destruction occurring right now through the materialism of the unfaithful.

Paul explained that the Corinthian church was inferior to others in the area of stewardship because he failed to discipline them in the support of his ministry. Some today try to disqualify Paul's teaching on tithing and giving because he didn't require strict obedience in Corinth for his personal support. But Paul asked them to forgive him this wrong as he reviewed how it had weakened them. "For what is it wherein ye were inferior to other churches, except it be that I myself was not burdensome to you? forgive me this wrong" (2 Corinthians 12:13).

Churches are still made inferior when they do not make the scriptural response to their responsibility to support the ministry God has ordained. It doesn't matter if the default is the preacher's fault or the member's; the resulting condition is an unavoidable consequence.

If we can recognize with Paul that poor stewardship handicaps the church, then we may also see that the individual is similarly affected. Disobedient stewards, whether from ignorance, covetousness or rebellion, will suffer spiritual dwarfism. They will miss out on the growth to which they are entitled. They will lack understanding, and they will not be entrusted with true riches. The ultimate negative consequence is that they may suffer spiritual death (Matthew 25:30).

Melchizedek Again

The first time God gave teaching directly on the subject

141

of tithing was in Genesis 14. He used Melchizedek, the strongest type of Christ in the Old Testament, to establish that tithing would always be an acknowledgment of the lordship of Christ.

Then in the last teaching on tithing in the New Testament, God used Melchizedek again, lest we forget the connection to Christ and the fundamentals essential to an understanding of this important practice. Now we can see that God anchored this vital teaching in Melchizedek in both covenants so that tithing arches over history, over the law and over the churches (Acts 7:38) of both the Old and New Testaments.

Melchizedek was a king (Hebrews 7:1). Jesus is King of Kings (1 Timothy 6:15). Melchizedek was high priest, and so is Christ (Hebrews 5:10). The Levitical priesthood was subordinate to Melchizedek when Abraham paid tithes (Hebrews 7:4-7). Everybody and everything became subordinate to Christ after His resurrection (Hebrews 7:28; 1 Corinthians 15:27). Jesus has the power of an endless life. The Father has called Him a priest forever after the order of Melchizedek (Hebrews 7:17, 21).

Hebrews 7:8 is a beautiful summary statement: "And here men that die receive tithes." When we bring the tithe of all the increase God has given us, it will be used to support those mortals whom God has called to minister in His church. "But there he receiveth them, of whom it is witnessed that he liveth." Concerning whom has the New Testament declared "that he liveth"? Jesus (Hebrews 7:16, 17, 24, 25, 28)! And where does the Bible tell us that Jesus now is seated? At the right hand of the Father (Revelation 3:21).

Now look at the marvelous revelation. Here mortal men receive tithes, but there (in heaven) He (Jesus) receives them "of whom it is witnessed that he liveth." The church is His body on earth (Ephesians 1:22, 23). He is the head over all things to the church (1:22; 5:23). Consequently, our bringing of tithes to the church (His body on earth) is also received by the head of the Body (our Lord Jesus Christ in heaven).

Tithing has always been to Jesus. There are many reasons

to tithe, as we have studied. But there is none greater than this: Jesus our Lord, who gave Himself for us, is honored and worshiped when we tithe . . . and He personally receives it. Think about that when you bring the tithe, and it will be a delight to you. You will be blessed . . . spiritually and materially . . . so you can be a blessing . . . to Christ and to your generation.

Conclusion

Perhaps you have not always been faithful to the Lord Jesus in bringing to Him the tithe of every increase He has entrusted to you. If after reviewing these Scriptures the Holy Spirit has convinced you of the importance of tithing, here is a prayer that will assist you with a fresh commitment.

Father in heaven, I thank You for saving me through the sacrifice of Jesus. I thank You for Your magnificent purpose for my life. I deeply desire to see Your purpose fulfilled in me. I am glad to be born again in Your image. I am delighted that obedience to Your Word produces Your likeness in me. Help me to be a faithful steward over all You entrust to me. Thank You for allowing me to participate in the family business—the church.

I confess to You that I have failed to obey Your Word in this important area of stewardship. Please forgive me this sin of disobedience. I commit to You now that I will promptly bring the tithe to the church where You have placed me every time You bless me with an increase. And please heal the hurts I have caused in the lives of others by my sin.

I thank You for the clarity of Your Word concerning tithing, giving and faithfulness. I praise You for Your wisdom to enable me to live as Your redeemed child in an unredeemed world through the power of Jesus' lordship over my life and resources. I praise You, Father, that You are my source. I refuse to worry. "The Lord is my shepherd; I shall not want." I rejoice to know that every time I worship You with tithes, the Lord receives it. I thank

You that through my obedient faithfulness I am honoring the Lord with my substance, and I will be blessed as I grow in my walk with You.

I confess Jesus as Lord with my mouth. I believe it in my heart. I demonstrate it with my deeds as Your faithful steward. I understand that I am blessed to be a blessing. Thank You, Father, for this wonderful relationship and for the joy of knowing You. In Jesus' name. Amen.

The Church Training Course Series

Proving God: Triumphant Living Through Tithing by Al Taylor has been designated in the Church Training Course program as CTC 407. The certificate of credit will be awarded on the basis of the following requirements:

1. The written review and instructions for preparing the review are listed on pages 123. The written review must be completed and evaluated by the pastor or someone he designates. Then the name of the student must be sent to the state office. (No grade will be given for the written review.)

2. The book must be read through.

3. Training sessions must be attended unless permission for absence is granted by the instructor.

4. The written review is not an examination. It is an overview of the test and is designed to reinforce the study. Students should search the text for the proper answers.

5. If no classes are conducted in this course of study, Church Training Course credit may be secured by home study.

A training record should be kept in the local church for each person who studies this and other courses in the Church Training Course program. A record form (CTC 33) will be furnished upon request from the state office.

WRITTEN REVIEW
Proving God: Triumphant Living Through Tithing/CTC 407

Instructions

1. A Certificate of Credit will be awarded when the student satisfies the requirements listed on page 121.

2. The student, at a time designated by the instructor, should search the test for the answers to the review questions. These should be written on a blank sheet of paper and presented to the instructor for processing.

3. In the case of home study, the student should present his answers to the pastor or to someone the pastor designates.

Questions

1. What was the original purpose for which God created you as stated in Genesis 1:26?

2. How did God giving of dominion (stewardship) to us affect the fulfillment of His magnificent purpose for us?

3. Explain the difference in God's position of ownership and man's position of stewardship?

4. Where in the Bible did God first teach us an understanding of tithing?

5. Identify two key components in Abraham's relationship with God that are essential for the principle of blessing to work in us.

6. Name as many parallels as you can between Melchizedek and Christ.

7. Why did Melchizedek serve bread and wine to Abraham?

8. What can the believer do to solve the problem of "filthy lucre" and "unrighteous mammom?" Give Scripture reference?

9. Name the first three feasts and describe their spiritual significance.

10. Show how the Feasts of Firstfruits relates to Christ and to the tithe.

11. What is the connection between the empty throne, the empty cross, the empty tomb and tithing?

12. Explain why the fulfillment of the law did not terminate the practice of tithing.

13. Compare man's efforts to have good luck through gambling and other superstitions as opposed to the blessing that comes through tithing.

14. Complete this sentence: "Faithfulness in tithing puts God first and is a powerful defense against_____."

15. Describe the three tithes discussed in chapter 7.

16. How can you refute the charge that tithing is legalistic?

17. The author says, "Discipline is the key to real freedom." How does this apply to stewardship?

18. Why did Jacob the deceiver receive God's blessing, while Esau could find no place for repentance?

19. How do we rebuke the "devourer" through tithing?

20. Jesus said to seek first the kingdom of God and His righteousness. How does that apply to stewardship?

21. My stewardship is a constant, outward revealing of where I am _____ in my walk with God.

22. Where does God give His final instructions on tithing in the New Testament?

23. Who receives the tithe on earth? in heaven?

24. Will tithing ever cease?

25. How many New Testament scriptures can you find which teach Christians to tithe? List them.

26. Do Christians testify that God blesses them for tithing? What is your testimony?